JANEEN R. BROWN

UNLEASH JOY

30 DAYS TO CLARITY, PEACE AND LONG-AWAITED HAPPINESS

ISBN: 978-0-9982038-3-6

Formatting Template Provided by

www.archangelink.com

Free Companion Workbook Download

More than 30 new exercises and transformational
questions designed to enhance your experience and guide your journey.

www.UnleashJoy.com/workbook

Dedication

To my loving husband Danger,
for being a teacher of mindful, loving touch, and a support in times when I forgot my divine nature.

To my children Zachery, Kirsten, Moyra, Amelie & River,
for reminding me that all I do is being watched by those who matter the most.

To my parents, Bob and Debi,
for the foundation on which I built my amazing joy-filled life.

Thank you

Contents

Mindset Practices

FOREWORD

It is said that happy people want to help everyone around them be happy, while unhappy people really don't want to be around people who are experiencing joy. Recently a friend posted on Facebook that she was tired of all the gratitude and happy posts on her Facebook feed because she feels that by encouraging others to be happy, we're robbing them of a true "human experience." Sadly, many people feel that they deserve their misery and that it's a worthwhile endeavor. These people feel that in suffering, they are feeling a range of emotion that makes them human. In addition to demanding that others embrace their misery, they revel in the sympathy that accompanies it. Misery is far easier to express than joy, and many people feel that since so many people are happy, their sadness is *what makes them special.*

While the human emotional range is indeed vast, it's also true that "to err is human". Surely we can agree that striving for joy is a worthy pursuit. In seeking happiness, we live our dreams, watch as our world becomes a wonderful place to live in, and we teach our children that adversity does not mean an end to joy. By wallowing in our sadness, we risk depression and even suicide. Our brain can become addicted to emotional suffering, just as it can to the strength of overcoming it. Which will you choose?

I remember when I first heard that you can "choose" to be happy. I didn't believe it. I said that depression was a mental condition that *required* medication. I realized later that I may just be a happiness Luddite, so I tried *telling* myself that I was happy. I tried saying that my life was amazing and filled with wonder, and I smiled at myself in the mirror even when I didn't feel like it.

You know what? I suddenly *felt* happier. It was working. I was *choosing* to be happy, and joy was flowing into my being.

In this book, you will find incremental changes, that when committed to, can improve a person's life in compounding, but subtle ways. The ten habits discussed in the first section will help you to change your environment and the way you feel about how things are manifesting in your life. The ten mindset changes in the second section are ways of viewing the world which can increase peace and clarity while better defining what you want. You can create the world around you, simply by deciding what you want in it, and then working to fill your world with that vision. The third portion of this book is a series of ten mindfulness practices that produce an abundant and joy-filled life. By integrating these mindfulness strategies, I have created a life full of small joys that have transformed my state of being from one of stress and anxiety to one of joy and peace.

While you may certainly read this book from front to back, feel free to open it up to any section and read only that portion, set it down and come back to it later. Enjoy reading the sections that appeal to you, or the ones calling for more clarity or attention in your life. Whether read from back to front, front to back, or in small increments, the chapters are simple and easy to read, and will help to unlock hidden joys and pleasures in your day.

Do not be afraid to live your life with clarity. The happiest people are those who make authentic decisions based on their higher wisdom and the light and love that flows from that source. In my personal experience, I have been happiest when living from this perspective. In each aspect of my life, whether parenting, my marriage, my writing, or my friendships I strive to be authentic as much as possible. This can mean breaking out of my comfort zone, discussion of things that make me vulnerable and asking for feedback from those around me so that I may improve.

In striving to be authentic, I've found that making small changes over time to determine my personal truth has been integral in my journey toward joy. I now regularly analyze my behavior and how it is in agreement or discord with my world view, and my beliefs. This practice has lead me on a path of clarity and a purpose-filled life. This book is full of questions you can ask yourself, habits you can create, and changes to your mindset, that will open your mind and allow your divine self-wisdom to come through.

Allow me to take you on my journey from depression and anxiety, panic attacks and medication, to peace and happiness. Allow me to show you how I learned to Unleash Joy.

Habits

Ten easy to implement daily habits, designed to set the foundation for joy.

"Your beliefs become your thoughts,
Your thoughts become your words,
Your words become your actions,
Your actions become your habits,
Your habits become your values,
Your values become your destiny."
- Mahatma Gandhi

"A man who can't bear to share his habits,
Is a man who needs to quit them."
- Stephen King, *The Dark Tower*

Day 1: Keeping It Real

I set the $10 bill on the table and headed to the kitchen. It was only for a few moments because I had intended to retrieve my purse from the bedroom after stirring the pot on the stove. The phone rang, however, and I forgot the money. Just as I finished cooking supper, my son Zachery came into the kitchen and asked me how many Star Wars figures he could buy for $10. I smiled knowingly, and told him he could probably afford a very nice one if he had $10, and I asked him how he had earned the money. He admitted finding the money on the table but didn't understand that it wasn't his. He made a great argument for finder's keepers, but in the end, I explained that his dream of a Star Wars figure would have to wait, and thanked him for admitting where he'd gotten the money. I then gave him a list of jobs he could do to earn the $10. He never did them.

"You must take personal responsibility.
You cannot change the circumstances,
the seasons, or the wind, but you can
change yourself."
- Jim Rohn

From birth, we are educated to believe that someone else is responsible for our personal growth, our education, our financial situation and even for our happiness. We're encouraged to play sports without keeping score (we're all just having fun, and everyone deserves to win), and since the 1980's our parents have been encouraged to work continually on improving our "self-esteem" so we can be happy. The result of this parenting philosophy is that we have generations of adults and young adults who feel entitled to a great life without being willing to work for it. While our parents had the lofty goals of giving their children better lives than they had, the result was that many of us feel we deserve that life without any effort on our part. While it's one of the hardest changes to make in our lives, you have to accept that your current predicament is a result of your actions and mental attitude, and no one else's.

I have wonderful memories of my childhood. We spent our summers camping and rock-hounding, and our winters tromping in Colorado snow and eating soup while watching The Cosby Show. We were poor, but relatively happy. As a small child, I strove to please my parents, but that became less relevant as I aged. There was a transition period when I needed to learn that if I wanted to accomplish something, it had to be for myself instead of for my parents or anyone else. The phase of my life where I was in that transition, was a difficult time for me. I remember my grades dropping, friendships waning, and being lost and confused, not knowing what I wanted or how to go about it even if I did.

Christmas was an especially difficult time of year for my father when money would be tight. His kids (my brother and I) would have lists of wishes, and he had a wife at home who hoped for a bigger house and nicer car. I remember him spending a lot of time in the garage during that time of year; quietly sequestered away, hoping that none of us would judge him for our poverty. I know he did his best, but sometimes, when you have a teenage girl that hasn't yet learned to appreciate what she has, life can be pretty hard on a man trying to make ends meet. I know I was difficult, especially during the holidays. I remember being continually ungrateful and resentful that we didn't have more. I'm so sorry, dad.

The year my father joined Amway things changed for him. I remember after a few meetings he came home and had a long talk, apologizing to my mother, brother and me for not being a better provider. It was a tear-filled moment of truth in our lives. I remember being incredibly proud of him. He started wearing a suit and speaking with a strength that I never knew he had. He also re-committed to his religious faith with new conviction. This one act of taking responsibility for his life, and working toward making a better future changed him in every way. His entire demeanor changed, and I saw him as a genuinely happy person for the first time.

It wasn't much later that I consciously decided to grow up and take responsibility for *my* actions. I was 19 years old, and I had a profound realization - that I wanted to be different. I remember having an idea of what a "good person" might be, what a kind mother, wife, and friend could be. I also recall realizing that I didn't fit into any of those categories. I had poor grammar, like many other children who grew up in that underpriveledged neighborhood in

Southern Colorado Springs, Colorado. I had gotten married just out of high school and had a baby *less* than nine months later. I had also lived in such a way that I hurt the people around me - parties and late nights, even after my son was born. I wasn't a particularly nice person, and I was incredibly selfish.

I had a lot of *excuses* for my behavior:

- I was young, just a child, and I wanted to have fun with my peers.
- My then-husband left me and joined the military and wasn't even in the country. I was lonely.
- I didn't know how to balance being a mother and being only 19.
- I was involved with the wrong group of people and didn't know how to find friends that would be supportive of a better lifestyle.

I needed an intervention, and I got it. The people closest to me gathered around and explained how I was on a path to self-destruction. They explained how I had hurt them, and how they were willing to support my growth and change. It was humbling.

While I would have told you that it was the "Worst day of my life" at the time, I realize now, many years later, that it was the BEST day of my life. I quit my job to get away from friends who were a bad influence, moved my belongings back in with my parents, and started over. It was a challenging journey, with a lot of self-reflection and a lot of apologies. The growth process began all those years ago and hasn't stopped. I continue to work on myself and my relationships, my contribution to the world and my personal titles of wife, mother, daughter and friend.

The painful experience of taking responsibility for *my* actions, whether good or bad, was one I'll never forget. While on the one hand it was painful and I felt shame and remorse, it was also freeing and empowering. I felt like all the advice, support, and examples I had all through my life were hitting me all at once. I finally realized that until I took responsibility for my choices, I couldn't hope to make better ones. I couldn't admit that there was a better way to live. I began learning how I could take the steps to change myself into the woman I wanted to be.

Responsibility is accepting that you are *both* the cause and the solution to the matter.

Responsibility is owning up to your choices. If you blame others for your situation, you torment those around you who take responsibility that belongs to you. If you make decisions without regard for responsibility, you are selfish and greedy. If you demand that you be cared for, given rewards or treated in a certain way without the responsibility of working toward that outcome, you are consumed with entitlement. The mindful choice, the one that leads to peace and healing, is responsibility. Own all of your decisions, past, and future. Acknowledge that your present predicament is the result of your previous actions.

- I got a flat tire because I didn't purchase new tires when the tread was worn.

- My front yard is full of weeds because I've not made buying grass seed and watering a priority.
- My child cannot yet read because I've not spent the time necessary to tutor them.
- My partner is distant because I've not shown them how important they are to me.
- I argue with my mother every time she visits because I choose to discuss things that upset her.

Taking responsibility is as simple as looking around, and admitting that "This is mine." I made this. I encouraged this behavior. I created this space. I had the bad attitude that made this day crummy. I didn't educate myself better. You are already responsible for everything around you, but acknowledging it is the first step in changing your life for the better. Once you take control of your choices and actions, admit that they are *yours* and yours alone, you can heal and move forward toward greatness.

There is an internet meme phrase for responsibility, "keeping it real." You can search for this phrase on nearly every social media site, and you'll see images and posts of people admitting fault, sharing messes they made or fender benders. You'll see that you're not alone - we all make mistakes, and no one has a perfect day, every day. Admitting what's yours, and "keeping it real" allows you to move forward with grace instead of pretending that anyone else is somehow responsible for your actions or your choices.

I made all the *choices* that got me to this moment.

Build the habit

Make a commitment today to take responsibility for your life. Accept that the actions you've taken in the past have lead you to this moment in time, to this body, this home, and this situation. Remember that positive change starts with acceptance of responsibility. Keep it real.

Day 2: Greet the Day

This girl CAN SLEEP. Seriously, it doesn't matter how much rest I've gotten; I can sleep 12-16 hours a day, easily. If I had no responsibility, I would be in hibernation. Getting out of bed has always been a challenge for me.

Not anymore. I tried going to bed early (yay, more sleep!) and getting into the habit of a bedtime routine. I know my WHY, and it's just not enough to get me out of those warm covers. But, I found something that is. I downloaded an app on my iPhone that makes me walk 30 steps before it shuts off. There were two kids in the bed with us this morning, so I had to rush out of the bedroom with my phone so as not to wake them with my crazy loud alarm. Then, the third child is in her room with her door open, so I had to go to the bathroom and walk around trying to figure out how to get this thing to shut up! I kid you not; it took me three tries to walk around the bathroom and get it to register my steps and finally turn off.

In the end, the app chimed and reported: "You are awake."

No kidding. Lol, I'm making coffee.

Good morning!

-A recent Facebook post.

"I am lucky; I don't have aches and pains.
I do Pilates regularly, which is a series of stretching exercises,
and I recommend it to anyone of my age because
the temptation is not to exercise when you get older. Well, you should."
- Ian McKellen

"Sometimes your joy is the source of your smile,
But sometimes your smile can be the source of your joy."
- Thich Nhat Hanh

"Keep your face always towards the sunshine,
And the shadows will fall behind you."
- Walt Whitman

Having a morning routine mapped out can be a true game changer. In this world of fast-paced technology, super stressed individuals and ever widening income disparity, it is essential that you have a ready plan for your morning to "set the stage" for what you are hoping to accomplish. Research any Fortune 500 company CEO, any billionaire or super-successful person and you'll find a deliberate morning that puts their mind and body in line for maximum achievement and minimum stress. Richard Branson, of Virgin, recently outlined his morning routine, and hopeful entrepreneurs the world over are clamoring to emulate him in hopes that some of his success will rub off. Richard's morning routine includes getting up early (so he can achieve more), meditating, reading, writing, exercise and spending time with his family. He cultivates a joyful and creative mindset, which he carries with him throughout the day. Let's discuss why you may want to implement some of these strategies in your own life, and just how you can do that.

* * *

Your body temperature lowers at night while you're sleeping as part of the natural circadian rhythm process. Bathing before bed helps you rest better for this very reason. As your body temperature lowers after a shower or bath, you naturally become drowsy. The reverse is true for waking. As your body temperature rises, you become more alert. Stretching your muscles first thing in the morning helps to warm your body and wake you up! I stretch out languidly just as I'm opening my eyes in the morning. I also do a few easy yoga positions, to warm up the muscles in my legs and lower back, and help relieve any aches I might have. Now that I'm in my 40's flexibility has become essential and I'm more aware of the toll of my past sedentary lifestyle. Beginning my day with stretching relieves tension and energizes my body for the day.

When I was younger, I took my body for granted. I was in denial of how things change as we age. I was surprised at 29 to find a gray hair, at 35 to feel a loss of energy and at 40 to start to feel aches and pains. I still feel like a kid inside! In high school I was voted "Most likely to age gracefully", and while I appreciate the sentiment today, back then it was a real blow. I had hoped for "Most likely to succeed" or "Most talented." Little did I know!

My morning stretch is the first message to and from my body for the day. It feels good, and as I stretch and release, I can feel my body responding and preparing to support me for the day. The morning stretch is a gift to my muscles, readying them for all I'll put them through during the day. After thanking my body for the rest it has provided, for the gift of another day, this stretch is a simple gift back. It increases blood flow to every part of my body and brings awareness of the day to every cell.

After getting up, one of the most important parts of my morning routine is exercise. I prefer to alternate between yoga and my treadmill, and I add strength training throughout the day. Being a busy mom, it's a challenge for me to fit in long workouts, so I do squats while I cook supper, calf raises while I home educate, and push ups while listening to my children practice their reading skills. They're watching me, and they stop to stretch, jump, push-up and squat on a regular basis too! I remember reading that one of my personal heroes - Ming-Na Wen, does squats and lunges in her kitchen when no one's looking! She's a fabulous actress, and her trim, fit physique at over 50 years old is commendable. I'm shooting for fabulous ME at 50!

Find an exercise program that you are comfortable with and speak with your doctor about starting the program. Do what you can, when you can, and rest and recuperate when you're not able to exercise. Loving your body, and moving and enjoying your muscles and joints, is one additional step in the path to joy. Feeling comfortable in your skin, always caring for your body and doing your best to maintain this miraculous machine that holds your soul is a way to tell yourself that you're worthy of health!

* * *

Smiling is amazing! Did you know that a simple smile can spread like wildfire? Smiles are contagious! Just watch a video of a baby laughing and smiling - It's so uplifting to see those happy little children giggling. Smiling uplifts everyone in the room, including yourself. It's truly a gift that you can give to everyone you meet, and it doesn't cost a thing. You sound more sincere if you smile while talking on the phone. Salespersons practice giving their pitches with a smile, and it works to increase sales. Smiling reduces stress and releases joy-producing endorphins.

As I stretch, I naturally smile. It's hard not to smile when you're doing something that feels so good! When we smile, we appear more confident and attractive to others. I'm *all* for looking more attractive first thing in the morning! I also find that smiling elevates my mood in the most natural and straightforward way. Go ahead and try it now - just smile. It brightens your eyes, lifts the muscles of your face and feels good. It also immediately helps to make the world around you a bit better. If you want to turbo-charge the effects of smiling, do it in the mirror!

* * *

The distance from the sun to the Earth is 92.96 million miles. When you feel the heat of the sun on your skin, you are feeling millions of miles of light. All that power from the one source at the center of our solar system is pouring out around us and traveling at 186,000 miles per second. It is immensely powerful energy. It feeds all living things on our planet and governs how our bodies regulate our work/rest schedule.

First thing in the morning, I can't wait to grab some sunlight on my skin. Especially my face. The light from the sun is welcoming and warm and fills me with a thrill to be alive. The energy from the sun is healing, and it reminds us of our celestial origins. Reflected in that powerful and radiant energy is my divine light, and I am reminded of that loving gift inside me when I feel the sunlight on my skin.

Several years ago, when my husband Danger and I were in the very bud of our relationship, I was stricken with a miscarriage. I didn't even know that I was pregnant. We decided not to notify our family so that no one would feel any kind of loss. At the time, I was hoping to simply set aside the emotional part of the circumstance and focus on my body's health and well-being. After about three days of cloistering up my feelings, a dam of pain burst and I couldn't get up out of bed. I seemed oblivious to the pain of loss, but a powerful sense of apathy and disinterest overtook me. I hardly ate or moved from my bed for almost a week. After trying to cheer me up with snuggles, comedy films, and chocolate, my husband picked me up from the bed and carried me outside onto the porch, blankets and all. Then, he just sat on our porch swing and held me in the sun. I finally broke down and cried, and the healing process began.

People living in the extreme North, where they spend many months of the year in darkness, suffer from increased rates of depression and anxiety. The "Winter Blues" or S.A.D. (Seasonal Affective Disorder), so named for the depression that sets in for many during the bleak winter months can be a real challenge for many people. If you suspect that you may suffer from S.A.D. consider light therapy or a vitamin D supplement. See www.unleashjoy.com/SADsolutions for my personal recommendations and additional references on this subject.

Sunlight notifies our body to shut off production of melatonin, the body's natural sleep-aid. Because of this, when you go outside first thing in the morning, or run to that sunny window and close your eyes, letting that warm light flow across your face, it wakes you up! Sunlight also works with our largest organ (the skin) to produce serotonin, the "motivation" molecule. It fills your body with energy and says "Good morning, life is beautiful!" in the most natural of ways.

Greeting the day with a bit of a stretch, a sweet smile, and some sunshine sends the message to your brain that life is beautiful, you are a gift, and today is going to be a fabulous day!

Build the habit

Stand up, stretch and smile. Open up those curtains, and get some sunlight on your skin. Open your mind and heart to the positive changes you're about to make toward joy! Make a habit of taking a breather outside, preferably first thing in the morning. Stretch your body and smile to begin your day with joy.

Day 3: Gratitude

He could tell by the set of my shoulders that something wasn't right. I may also have indicated it by my restless stance, biting nails and pained look on my face. He'd been in his office for hours, and while he was sequestered, I struggled to get the kids to clean up a few messes (while they created a few additional ones), broke an egg on the floor and dumped an entire can of cocoa powder down the side of my white refrigerator. In addition, I was facing canceled plans from someone I missed dearly and had just that morning spilled coffee into my computer keyboard, which no longer functioned. I'm such a lucky girl. He came up to me and hugged me. Then he looked into my eyes and asked the question I most needed to hear: "What's happening right now, that's good?" I listed our health, our amazing marriage, our beautiful daughters who were playful and happy, the produce from our garden and more. The more I listed, the better I felt. With every good and happy recognition, the wonder that is my life was made clear to my stressed soul, and my day healed.

"Gratitude is the healthiest of all emotions.
The more you express gratitude for what you have,

The more you will have to express gratitude for."
- Zig Ziglar

If you only read one chapter in this book, and especially if you only implement one of the 30 days of advice I'm giving…let it be this one. This transformational habit is so simple, so easy and so fast - but it is the most game-changing highway to joy that exists. There are two words, which, if said every day, first thing in the morning, and repeated whenever things seem rough will instantly move your mind from one of self-pity to empowerment and joy. Those words are:

THANK YOU

Gratitude is the secret ingredient to happy living. It's like the cinnamon in my chili (not so secret anymore, is it, dad?). Gratitude surprises me, even now that I practice it daily. I have my husband to thank for that. On the rare occasion that I'm stressed or down, he comes up and puts his hands on my shoulders and looks into my eyes, and lists three or four little things to be grateful for. My inner critic makes a feeble attempt at the three stages of pouty face (denial, pout some more, anger, pout some more, resignation, crack a smile) and my mind shifts from whatever I perceive as not working out for me at the time - to what IS. My mood is elevated, my heart is buoyant again, and I can breathe. The one thing you always have control over is your attitude!

Every morning I wake up, and I am thankful. There is always

something to be thankful for. I often have a child sprawled out on top of me, feet and limbs pressing against my spine, or hair in my face. I lean into that sweet child and inhale them a bit. Oh, it's so easy to be thankful for children! Gratitude comes easy when your life is filled with so many blessings. What then, can we be thankful for when life has handed us a few lemons? Johnny Cash once expressed thankfulness for a well-worn pair of shoes that fit his feet nicely. Abraham Lincoln reminded us to be thankful that "thorn bushes have roses" and Dame Judy Dench points out that you should be thankful to have employment when so many do not. Life is full of wonderful gifts, even at times when it can be nearly unbearably harsh. The sunshine on our skin, the mesmerizing flow of clouds across the sky, the sound of water flowing, are all things to appreciate.

When I was preparing to deliver my daughter Moyra 9 years ago, I remember using a program called Hypnobabies® to relax during labor. After a couple of days of training, my husband needed only to put his hand on my shoulder and whisper "peace" and my whole body would instantly relax and calm. It felt incredible. All the tension would just melt from my whole being. That's what gratitude does! It's like a magician, twirling silver balls in one hand, distracting you from the doves in his pocket. It removes your attention from negative things in your life and, like a light switch flipping, joy just flows into your mind, flooding out all negative thought.

Like attracts like, and gratitude attracts MORE of whatever you are thankful for. If you are lonely, be grateful for the friendly relationships you have. If you want a bigger, more beautiful home, first be thankful for the small one you have. LOVE it. Treat it with love. If you are struggling financially, first feel gratitude for those pennies in your pocket, the clothing you are wearing and the roof over your head. More of what you love will come to you.

Robert A. Emmons Ph.D. is working at the University of California, Davis to uncover the science and biology behind gratitude. His numerous studies have shown that gratitude is one of the most important components of human health and well-being.

Adult subjects in his studies who practice gratitude regularly and keep a gratitude journal, experienced:

- An increase in optimism
- Better physical health and wellness
- Greater goal achievement
- A boost to alertness
- More determination
- Increased energy

Children he studied experienced:

- A greater closeness to their families
- Increased appreciation for loved ones
- More enjoyment from their academic studies

I credit gratitude for my fabulous marriage. Instead of nagging each other, or pointing out little faults (we are human, after all), my husband and I choose to focus on constantly appreciating each other, verbally and mindfully. If ever we have a disagreement, we focus on gratitude, communication and love. Our marriage is secure and uplifting. After ten years, we're both still looking out the window, waiting for the other to get home from an errand. We still meet each other at the door with hugs and kisses after being absent for any amount of time. And yes, there's still that pitter patter of my heart when he's near.

When my eldest daughter reached an angsty 14 years old, it seemed like a stranger had moved into our home and taken over her body. She was grumpy and inconsolably frustrated. Small irritations turned into arguments, especially between her and her older brother. It was hard on her but turned into a rough time for our whole family. My husband and I came up with a plan to relieve the tension. We had a gratitude "hot seat" that rotated every night at supper. One person would be on the receiving end while everyone in the family would express gratitude or appreciation for that person in turn. Our parents thought it was such a good idea that they participated by phone. Everyone agreed that it felt good to be appreciated and affirmed by the other members of the family, and tensions eased soon after. On one occasion, my husband received gracious comments from my parents on his ability to provide through entrepreneurial endeavors online. Our son learned that his little sisters appreciated his silly, loud, playful attitude. And my daughter Kirsten heard how much we all loved and appreciated her, day after day. She in turn, was encouraged to express gratitude at a time when inside she felt all was a bit bleak. It healed her. She is grown and out of the house now, and our relationship is better than ever. Gratitude helped that angsty teen turn into an empowered woman.

You can implement a gratitude "hot seat" at home or work. Pick a co-worker or family member each day and say something like "I really admire the way you ________ every day." They don't need to know about the "hot seat" for it to work. It can be our secret!

Implementing gratitude in your life is as easy as listing three things you are grateful for. I do it first thing in the morning. Firstly, I'm always thankful for one more day. Secondly, I'm grateful for my life, the people in it, and my home. Third, I'm thankful for my goals, my drive and living my life's purpose. All of these things have fallen into place for me because I live the content of this book. I'm sharing it all with you in an effort to help bring *you* the joy I feel, so that when you wake up after these 30 days, gratitude flows from you easily; and your mind, your life, the people around you, the entire world, screams JOY!

Build the habit: Today, say "Thank you." Find at least three things to be thankful for. Tomorrow, and every day thereafter begin your day with gratitude. Thank you, Thank you, Thank you! Gratitude statements can be quite simple, like "I am alive.", "I slept in a warm bed last night.", or even "The sky is a lovely shade of blue." FEEL the thankfulness.

Avoid turning gratitude into a reluctant "Sigh..well, I guess things could be *worse*." Attitude. This viewpoint could be a dangerous slope toward despair. Instead, feel how thankful you are for even the little things in life. Begin to notice how small things can lead to immense joy. My five-year-old couldn't be happier chasing a butterfly across the lawn, or finding an interesting pebble in a gravel driveway, or quietly touching the rivulets in the bark of a tree. Remembering that simple curiosity about the world, and discovery of how even tiny pleasures can bring long-awaited happiness, can lead us to a simpler, yet more joyful life. Recall a happy memory, touch that favorite coffee cup, or put on those comfy yoga pants.

Build the habit

If you really want to kick-start the gratitude magic, sit down immediately and write 100 things you are thankful for. It is a POWERFUL exercise for positive change in your life!

Day 4: Your Torch Running Task

I watched as they loaded the back of the pickup truck. Five large black trash bags, seven boxes and several large items that included shelves, an easel, storage tubs and more. It was the third load this summer, and my recently-divorced girlfriend would be placing the items in a garage sale to earn some much-needed cash. I sat on the porch after she'd driven away, and thought of all I had accomplished. In just a short time, I had removed so much from our home that we never used, didn't like, and hadn't enjoyed for some time. Our house was cleaner, more open and free, and we were all happier for my efforts. I did it all one day at a time, one item at a time. In small increments, I transformed our home and helped a friend in the process.

"The hardest part of any important task,
Is getting started on it in the first place.
Once you actually begin work on a valuable task,
You seem to be naturally motivated to continue."
- Brian Tracy

Today is a new day. You wake up, look around and your To Do list floods into your brain. As a stay-at-home mom, I might have laundry, dishes, meal planning and cooking, home educating, gardening, cleaning, home improvement, seasonal preparations, holiday and party planning, etc. on my list. Life is busy! It can seem overwhelming to face a long list of things that all need to be done at once! Until we're all granted magical wands, robots or self-cleaning toilets, we're going to have to face our To Do list and take the steps necessary to work through it.

Working moms and dads have *two* lists to contend with. One at home and one at work! I remember my drive to work, years ago, when I'd transition from worrying about everything I had to do at home, to worrying about all I needed to accomplish at work. The whole process would reverse at the end of the day. It was a lot of worries to be carrying around! I don't know how I got it all done back then. I stay home now, and my To Do list is HUGE. I can't imagine how working moms get it all done!

The truth is, no one CAN get it all done. There will always be more dishes, another load of laundry and floors to be swept. However, for many of us, unfinished tasks may lead to thoughts of frustration, self-pity or inadequacy. Even though we know that others are struggling with the same frustrations, it doesn't help us cope with the seemingly insurmountable list of things to be taken care of, cleaned and completed. I've found that it helps tremendously to write down everything that needs to be done, at the end of the work shift or end of the day. Just to unload all the tasks that are outstanding, allows me to rest for the remainder of the evening, and sleep better at night.

To Do lists give you the benefit of checking things off as you accomplish them, which feels fantastic! Jack Canfield recommends keeping a journal of your successes, and a fully crossed-off To Do list can certainly represent a successful day! But how often do we finish everything on our task list for the day? I remember feeling frustrated as a new home educator, that I had planned a great week full of experiments, rewarding and challenging assignments and art projects. At the end of the week, we'd only gotten through about one-third of what I'd planned! I felt that it must have been something I was doing wrong, some flaw in my methodology. I talked to my mother-in-law, who is a retired school teacher. She told me that I had the same experience as every public school educator. They all over-plan and then do what they can.

Let's look at our day again. Knowing that there is a good possibility that you can't accomplish everything on your list, how can you finish the day feeling accomplished and successful? I can tell you that there IS a technique that can help you to feel fabulous at the end of the day, even though you didn't check off every item on your To Do list.

Every four years, eleven women gather at the Temple of Hera in Olympia, Greece for an ancient and powerful ceremony. These women herald the beginning of the world Olympic games. During their ceremony, they light the Olympic torch with sunlight alone, concentrated with a parabolic mirror. They then take the torch to Panathinaiko Stadium where they hold a celebration of victory, strength, and accomplishment, before the torch begins its journey to the host city for the Olympic Games.

One step at a time, the torch is carried to the games. All along its route, the flame remains lit - the symbol of hope and accomplishment for all to see. It is a great inspiration to aspiring athletes and a reminder of the rewards of hard work and perseverance.

If you imagine all your tasks as small steps toward great achievement, each representative of effort, of importance and our time's effectiveness, you can clearly see that one job outshines the others, or must be done *first*. That is your Torch Running Task.

If you only accomplished one task today, what would that be?

Identify your torch running task, and get it done first. That's the answer! Just pick the most important thing of all. The one task that you absolutely MUST do today. The one exercise or accomplishment that would rocket you closer to your goals, fulfill your personal mission statement, and provide the most satisfaction. It's usually the biggest, hardest, most challenging thing on your list, but it can be as simple as a phone call, or cleaning a single room. I usually have three things, one for home education, one for my household and one for my writing and coaching services. If you work, you might have one torch running task at home and one at work.

Now here's the real key to making this torch running task work. You have to do it FIRST. Just like the women in Olympia, this is the beginning of a great journey. You have to get it out of the way so that you can get on with the *rest* of your day. I know that the torch running task might be intimidating, messy or uncomfortable. It may have been on your list for the past three weeks, and you've just been putting it off. You *know* that when it's over and done with, things will be better. You know that having that unfinished task on your list is causing you a lot of pain - so get it over with already! Nike® says "Just Do It!"® and they are right!

- Call a company and negotiate the repayment of your bill (It won't be as bad as you think).
- Set a timer for 25 minutes and clean the top rack in your refrigerator (Do one shelf each day, and it won't be so bad).
- Apologize for something.
- Invite someone over.
- Confront a problem.
- Write, sing, practice your violin, upload a video to YouTube, just do the thing that will most rocket you toward completion of your goals NOW!

Completing the torch running task that is most important is how you take control of the day and make the change necessary to improve your life, one task at a time. This does not mean that you complete one task to the exclusion of everything else on your list. It means that you focus on the most important thing, and get it out of the way. Take a deep breath and move on to the next most important thing, and so on. At the end of the day, if you're not satisfied with your level of productivity, you'll at least see that you've done what was most important. You will be that much closer to achieving your goals, that much closer to your dream home, well-educated children, playing that sonata, finishing your book, etc.

Your first task of the day (after your morning routine) should be the torch running task. Make sure that it's doable, that it continues your momentum of positive achievement, and that you have all the necessary resources to complete the job. I like to do the torch running task for my career immediately after my morning routine. I complete the torch running task for home education between 8 AM and noon. Then I do the torch running task for my homemaking after lunch. I most certainly get more than three things done every day, but these three things make all the difference for me.

Every night, when I'm preparing my To Do list for the next day, I circle the one thing in each area that I really must get done the next day. For my business, it's nearly always writing, blogging, or video/ audio creation. For my home, it ranges from laundry to renovating or gardening. For my children, it's often reading lessons or working intimately with one of my girls on something that they're struggling with, or talking to my children about a habit I'd like them to form or a character trait we're encouraging.

Whatever your torch running task is, make time to get it done first, and your day will run much more smoothly. You'll be able to go to bed feeling accomplished, and you'll move that much closer to achieving your goals, which feels amazing!

Build the habit

Get out your To Do list, and write down the torch running task you will commit to doing today, that will make the greatest difference in your life. Then, without hesitation, DO IT. Every evening before bed, write your new To Do list for the following day. You can do this!

Day 5: Goal Setting

I heard someone shout "Ok, that's the last nail!" and a round of cheering and hollering ensued. We jumped and hugged and high-fived for several minutes until the young couple sheepishly approached their new front door. President Jimmy Carter stood on the front step, a Bible and house keys in his hand. He met the teary couple and their two small children, shook each of their hands and said something I couldn't quite hear. The man accepted the book and keys, and his wife hugged the former president on impulse - surely an act outside of decorum but welcomed none-the-less. Another round of cheering as the family entered their home for the first time. My company had asked for volunteers to spend a weekend building a house in Watts, California. I volunteered even though I was nearly seven months pregnant with my eldest daughter, and had no idea that there would be riots in less than 24 hours due to the Rodney King incident. We had to ride to the site in buses with darkened windows for our safety. We built an entire house in two days. President Carter's eyes widened a bit when he reached me, after shaking hands with 30 or so other volunteers. He held my hand and smiled, and thanked me for volunteering when I should be "resting on the couch." It was terribly sweet, and I felt proud to have accomplished such a meaningful goal and to be surrounded by so many other giving souls.

> "People with clear, written goals
> Accomplish far more, in a shorter period of time,
> Than People without them
> Could ever imagine."
> - Brian Tracy

Everyone sets goals. Even if they don't actively call what they're doing "goal setting". They participate in New Years resolution posts on Facebook and join 30-day fitness challenges. They make plans for their future and spend time dreaming of what could be. The problem is, even though we're all relatively accustomed to making goals, few of us are in the practice of completing them!

Most people simply want a better life for themselves and their children. Unfortunately, we get in our own way when it comes to achieving that better life. We allow ourselves to remain sedentary and never take the steps necessary to achieve our goals and find that "better life" we're all dreaming about. Worse, we complain about people who HAVE done what *we* wish we could do. The class warfare in our society encourages us to publicly lambaste and punish successful people, and scream about the "unfairness" of their success. What we're really saying is that we want to punish the most successful, hardest working, highest achieving, smartest people in our society. What kind of message does that send our children about their ability to achieve their own goals or their attitudes toward wealth?

It's widely known that goal setting is a useful tool for achieving your dreams. Reading and writing your goals on a daily basis is essential for keeping your future dreams in your conscious mind so that you absolutely *cannot* forget them. You can't ignore the elephant in the room, when that elephant is your dream come true, just waiting around the corner for you to get up and take action.

There is a popular myth that 3% of Harvard business graduates make more than the other 97% combined, due to goal setting. In the (mythical) groundbreaking phenomenal study done in 1979, researchers asked recent graduates of the Harvard MBA program if they had written goals for their future. Of the graduates, 84% had no written goals, 13% had mental goals but had not written anything down, and only 3% had clear, well-written goals and plans to achieve those goals. Ten years later, the same scientists interviewed the graduates again regarding their achievements since leaving Harvard. Interestingly, the 13% who had mental goals were earning twice as much as their peers that had not determined any specific goals at all. Double earnings!! Even more surprising, the 3% that had written goals and a plan to achieve those goals were earning, on average, ten times more than the other 97% *combined*.

Interestingly, the *true* study, done by Gail Matthews at the Dominican University of California in 2007, confirmed the above results. Her research showed that people who wrote down their goals accomplished significantly more than those who did not. The study provided empirical evidence for the effectiveness of coaching tools like accountability and commitment, as well.

You can't change the past, but you can change who you are today.

Today you can ask yourself "What exactly do I *want*?". You can take that answer and turn it into goals, and you can reverse-engineer those goals to visualize the steps needed to achieve them. In five years, you can reassess your behavior, and you can either regret not changing, not taking the first necessary step, or you can jump with joy at the fantastic progress you've made. Goal achievement is extraordinarily *simple*, but it isn't particularly *easy*.

Goal setting, when done *right*, can be incredibly powerful. When you take the time to ask yourself what you want for your future, without the baggage of thinking about anyone else, you'll be surprised by the depth and magnitude of what you want. When you dig even further into your vision to see how your goals can coincide with the betterment of the Human Race, *then* you've found your life's purpose. You find more than just personal desire, but a destiny that you were created for! When you get past the material needs and desires (better house, car, clothes, money for eating out, awesome job) and the physical (thin body, fit body, attractive body) you're left with the tougher desires that are spiritual or emotional (more friends, deeper understanding of self & my place in the universe, what is divine?) and then you finally ask the really tough questions like "What am I meant to contribute?", "How am I special?", "What kind of legacy can I leave?".

The question then arises, "How do you set achievable goals?" Since as early as 1981, self-help practitioners have been recommending the S.M.A.R.T. method of goal setting:

Specific
Measurable
Achievable
Relevant
Time-Sensitive

Specific goals are detailed and clearly written. It's easy for someone to say that they would like to write a book "someday", but that wouldn't be a useful goal because it lacks the details necessary to get you into the achievement mindset. A better-written version of this goal would read "I'm going to write a post-apocalyptic fiction novel", or better yet "I am writing a post-apocalyptic fiction novel." Using the words "I am" is a promise to yourself, and sends a clear message to your subconscious mind that you are ready to take action toward your goal.

Measurable goals add further detail to our already specific desire. Adding a measurement takes our goal from drab to fab! That may sound silly, but adding a measurable element guarantees a goal that is more than mediocre. Adding to the previous example, our goal becomes "I am creating a best-selling post-apocalyptic fiction novel of 90,000 words."

Achievable goals are realistic. If you turned your above goal into something a bit unrealistic, it might read "I am creating a New York Times best-selling post-apocalyptic, romance, vampire fantasy novel of 90,000 words that makes my readers turn into magical flying unicorns!" This example is obviously unattainable, but I've met many people who purposefully write goals that are unrealistic due to a fear of success, an ignorance of their niche (its laws, required education, or even knowing if it's something they'd like doing), or simply because they think goal setting is silly or ineffective. Do not take this as license to sell yourself short and write goals that are so small and easily achievable that they lose their meaning. Your goals should be just big enough to challenge you and make you feel both excitement and fear when you read them, but not impossible for you to achieve. Indeed, push yourself as much as you are able without going over the achievable "edge".

Relevant goals match your dreams. They are in line with your personal values, the hopes and dreams you have for your family and the hope you have for the future of this planet. Make your goals worthy of pursuit! I've seen many young people create goals based upon what their parents want from them, but not based on their own dreams and desires. Our parents want good things for us, and would like to see us succeed. However, if we don't design our path, we run the risk of feeling resentful or unfulfilled. Let's take a look at a new version of that goal we're creating. It now reads "I am writing a best-selling post-apocalyptic fiction novel that details the dangers of nuclear war and encourages readers to think about foreign policy. It will be 90,000 well-written words, in a style that appeals to young adults who will be making government policy in the future."

The last step in creating goals that work is to add time sensitivity. When our goals have a due date, our mind begins processing what needs to happen between now and that date to accomplish the goal. Adding a deadline holds us accountable and sets us on an immediate path to goal completion. Our finished goal will read: "I am writing a best-selling post-apocalyptic fiction novel that details the dangers of nuclear war and encourages readers to think about foreign policy. It will be 90,000 well-written words, in a style that appeals to young adults who will be making government policy in the future. The first draft will be ready for editorial review by December 31st."

After you write your awesome goals, it's time to reverse-engineer them. Imagine you're a scientist that has just discovered alien technology. Your job is to take it apart, figure out piece-by-piece how it works, and learn how to recreate it from scratch. You can process your goals similarly. Take a look at that due date and figure out how many days, weeks, months, or years you have to complete your goal. Then determine what needs to be done each day, week, month or year in order to complete your goal by the given due date. At the time of this writing, the current date is October 5th. If I were to begin today, I would have 87 days to write this novel, and I'd need to write approximately 1035 words per day to finish the novel by December 31st.

Lastly, I would add action steps to my To Do list, making "Write at least 1035 words in my awesome novel" as my torch running task for each day to knock this goal out of the park!

Build the habit

Take out a piece of paper and ask yourself "What do I want?" Start writing your "I want" list, and don't stop until you know you've hit the jackpot of personal desire for yourself - the dream that aligns with your spirit and makes you light up from the inside out. Then write S.M.A.R.T. goals that will get you what you want, and break them down into action steps. Add your first torch running task to your To Do list for tomorrow! As a daily habit, review your goals in light of your torch running task for the day. Keep a record of your victories!

Day 6: Three Chores for a Happy Home

My 9-year-old self couldn't imagine a better place to take a nap than on my Aunt Lennie's bed. Her bedroom was tidy, minimalist and fancy. The sheets and duvet were a gold satin, and she had one of those oil droplet lamps in the corner. My aunt was always such a classy dresser. Opening the 1970's mirrored cork sliding doors to her closet revealed tidy rows of heeled shoes and boots, and beautifully pressed slacks and blouses hanging above. During each of our family visits to her home, I always made an excuse to "nap" on Aunt Lennie's bed. I enjoyed lying there and daydreaming about how my future home and future bedroom would look. Though my home is nothing like hers was, I can say that she has inspired me. Just not to the point of buying one of those dated oil lamps on Ebay.

"I know that birds have little birds,
And fish have little fishes.
Then why don't sinks have little sinks,
Instead of dirty dishes?"

- Unknown

"If you make your bed in the morning,
You will have accomplished the first task of the day.
By the end of the day, that one task completed
Will have turned into many tasks completed.
And if by chance you have a miserable day,
A made bed gives you encouragement that tomorrow will be better."
- Admiral William H. McRaven, U.S. Navy SEAL

"No matter how bad your day was,
Just remember that someone out there
Has to clean the bathrooms at Taco Bell."
- Unknown

Chores never end. There is always something to clean, laundry to do, dishes to wash. If you have children, the mess is multiplied until it feels as though you're merely "holding back the tide" and never really gain any ground. One mess leads to more, and before you know it your clutter is having babies! I have five children, two of whom have moved out to join the world, and thankfully took most of their belongings with them! The remaining children, three darling little girls, are a never-ending source of both joy and chaos. As a mother, I'm tasked with not only keeping my home clean and tidy but also creating a space that evokes peace and harmony. If our space doesn't reflect this, everyone in the home can suffer.

It's difficult to get it all done. Some days we downright fail at keeping our homes in any way presentable. I remember struggling with constant feelings of frustration and failure. As my children have grown, I've been able to involve them more in helping to keep our home neat. I've also learned which three chores made the most difference in our home, and how I felt about my space. These three chores not only help my home to have an air of beauty and cleanliness, but they fill me with peace and tranquility. While they may seem simple or rudimentary to some, many people who are never taught the art of keeping house need to know where to start in order to make their house feel like a *home*.

* * *

It is hard to believe there was a time in my life that I didn't clean my kitchen in the evening. Waking up to a dirty kitchen must be one of the most depressing things in the universe. Not only is it a stark reminder of the long list of things you need to do today, it's a representation of what you didn't accomplish the day before. Walking into that space, the one where you lovingly create nourishing meals for your family and seeing a mess and unclean dishes only fills you with feelings of guilt and shame. You deserve better! I want to start my day with pride and joy. I want that room to represent only love and peace so that I can create meals that nourish bodies *and* souls.

Every night after supper, the kids clean the table. One empties the dishwasher while another puts silverware away, and a third takes out the trash. I get the children prepared for sleep and then set myself up to clean my kitchen. I usually put on headphones and listen to an audio book, TED talk, or an inspirational podcast. I put myself wholly into cleaning the kitchen, knowing that I'm creating a space that will be a gift to my future self - the Janeen of tomorrow, who will wake up and be thankful for what she sees. The woman who will walk into my kitchen, turn on the kettle and look around her with a sense of peace instead of guilt and regret.

I wash the dishes and load the dishwasher. Any dishes that don't fit or need to be cleaned by hand are washed, dried and put away. I clean my sink, counters, my stove, and I give the cabinets and appliances a quick swipe. This takes me approximately 30 minutes to complete but provides hours of pleasure the next morning. Since I usually begin my day with meditation, affirmations, and positive visualization, waking to a clean kitchen allows my mind to be free and calm, without the weight of responsibility and unfinished tasks. Having that peace first thing in the morning, lasts throughout my day, allowing me to cultivate mindfulness and patience as I home educate, cook, tidy up and work on my writing.

* * *

Every morning, one of the first tasks of my day is to make my bed. That wasn't always the case. I remember feeling that there was little point in making my bed if I were only going to mess it up again that night. True, my bedroom was drab, and I would often pile things on my bed instead of putting them away. I never felt my bedroom was "pretty" or even comfortable. I certainly didn't take pride in it.

Then something interesting happened; I discovered Pinterest. If you've not visited this website yet, you're in for a treat. It's been called "Catnip for women" and is incredibly addictive. I warn that it's best not to use the site if you don't have an hour or two to waste! Personally, I've had nothing short of a fantastic experience with it. Not long into my first day on Pinterest, I started perusing images of home decor. It became my vision board. 500 pins and 2 hours later, my mind was filled with images of beautifully decorated master bedrooms. I wanted that! I wanted my bedroom to be *pretty*! I hopped on Amazon and bought my first matching bedding. When it arrived I was incredibly pleased. I made my bed happily for the first time since living with my parents!

My husband Danger, is *not* a decorative pillow kind of guy, but he went along with my room transformation and admitted to liking how our bedroom looked and felt. That first day, I peeked into my bedroom several times and took at least five photographs of my beautiful bed. I felt pride in my bedroom for the first time. In the days following, I noticed not only a change in the way I felt about that one room but also in the way I felt about the rest of my home. I wanted the whole house to be pretty. I wanted more than ever for it to be tidy and well-decorated. I got rid of three truckloads of clutter that month, largely due to how that bedding made me feel!

My bedroom has become a haven of peace and tranquility for me. At any point throughout my day, if I'm feeling stressed or overwhelmed, I can take five minutes in my bedroom, admire that lovely space and breath peace and patience back into my being. I simply walk by that room and smile, knowing that there is a part of my home that feels truly lovely. I look forward to winding down and getting ready for bed, conscious that this beautiful and peaceful place is waiting for me to come lay my head and rest.

* * *

What is the one room that guests will judge you the most for? The one place that they require privacy and cleanliness? Yes, it's the bathroom. With three little girls, I *know* how hard it is to keep the bathroom clean during the day. I swear that my kids make plans to sneak into the bathroom at least three times per day, and create a flood of biblical proportions. Naked Barbie™ bubble parties, a slick floor, barrettes strewn all over and misplaced hand towels are the norm, with plugged drains, mud, or strange smelling or colored liquid science experiments being only occasional occurrences.

Not only does a dirty bathroom make us feel uncomfortable, but it can be a health hazard as well. In addition, it will make guests feel awkward and question the safety and cleanliness of the rest of your home (and even question whether or not they should eat your food). If you are feeling overwhelmed at the state of your home, this is the room to start in. In just a few minutes you can pick up this small space. Taking 5 minutes first thing in the morning to "swish and swipe" as The Flylady® recommends, by taking the brush to your toilet and wiping down the vanity, you'll have a sweet-smelling clean room in no time.

Every time I use my restroom I take a few moments and pick up before I leave. I do my best to curtail any natural disasters that my kiddos cook up in there. I work in small increments to keep that room, above all others, in decent shape. I maintain the cleaning supplies under the sink so I can clean up any messes quickly without ever having to leave that room. I clean the mirror and disinfect the door, toilet and faucet handles once per day. It only takes a few minutes to take care of this room, but it makes a huge difference to a guest and helps to keep my family healthy.

My home only has one restroom, which makes it doubly important that I keep this room clean. If anyone in our home becomes ill, it is imperative that I make sure germs don't spread to the rest of the family. Living in close proximity makes it challenging to keep illness from spreading, but by maintaining the cleanliness of the bathroom, I can mitigate that risk. In addition, I dispose of old medications and keep any dangerous drugs or toiletries out of reach of children. I would never want to be responsible for a visiting child's ingestion of something harmful in my home.

In keeping my bathroom tidy, I can reduce the stress that I might otherwise have when I receive a surprise visitor. I feel comfortable in my bathroom and know that I have helped my guests feel that way too. This one action helps put forth a good impression of the rest of my home to anyone visiting.

Build the habit

Take the time immediately after supper to wash all the dishes and clean your kitchen. Make your bed today! If you are able, invest in a handsome set of matched bedding to motivate you to keep your bed made. Enjoy this peaceful space, and take advantage of it throughout the day. Work to pick up your bathroom and keep it tidy every time you utilize that room. Small, incremental steps keep this important room clean and safe. Your future self will thank you!

Day 7: Scheduling

I looked down at the piece of paper on my desk. Hours before, I had printed out a tentative schedule for the day, just to try it. I stood there in awe at all I'd accomplished. Laundry, tidying the bathroom, living room and dining room, homeschool, and two phone calls. We'd had breakfast and lunch. Everyone had real clothes on and hair brushed, and it wasn't even 2 PM. I knew that I'd discovered a way for me to feel accomplished at the end of every day. I finally had the means to get it all done. If I'd only known how simple it was, I would have done it years ago.

> "The key is not to prioritize your schedule,
> But to schedule your priorities."
> - Stephen Covey

Scheduling is an excellent way to guarantee a focus on your goals and the things that matter most to you. More importantly, you'll not end your day feeling regretful about how you spent your time. You will have taken control of your time and used it according to your plan, instead of being a slave to life's punches. When you plan your day, urgent things no longer take time from important things. Scheduling allows you to make time for spiritual growth, meditation or prayer. Exercise is no longer forgotten because you "didn't have time" for it. A new mother can schedule time for her shower, meal planning, and housecleaning. Scheduling can allow time for gardening, home educating children, writing that book you've always wanted to write, working on a home business, and even spending time with your partner. At the end of the day, you can reflect on exactly how you've spent your time.

Scheduling can relieve a tremendous amount of stress. It's so much easier to handle tasks that are familiar and routine. The biggest relief is not going to bed with regret. You will also discover the joy of not having to make decisions all during the day on how best to spend your time (or how our children should be spending theirs). By starting with a firm plan for your day, everyone knows *what* to expect, *when* to complete each task and how much time they have before they need to change activities. Because you'll be more productive with your schedule, emergency situations can come without you feeling that the entire day has been wasted. Doctor appointments become just a part of the schedule, and a surprise visit in the afternoon still means that the morning was successful. The person who plans their day doesn't feel overwhelmed, overloaded or overworked - everything has its time, or place and it actually gets *done*. You can be more mindful and patient with your children because you've relieved a great deal of your burden. A schedule is a blessing to the whole family, reducing stress and bringing peace every hour.

For me, scheduling is an absolute necessity. I home educate three daughters of different ages. I cook a traditional whole food diet, with no processed food, and I even grind wheat and bake bread. I garden, clean, do dishes and numerous other chores to keep my home clean. I'm also writing this book (I'll likely be working on another at the time you're reading this), writing in my blog, professionally speaking and coaching. Then there's the development on the back-end of that business, the website maintenance, book covers, working with editors, and more! If I didn't have a schedule, I wouldn't get a quarter of that done!

Ask yourself what you would like to have time to do. If you could just squeeze in 15 - 30 minutes, or an hour, what would you do with that time? You would be surprised how much time is available to you if you schedule. I schedule nearly everything, including time for social media. I find that if I don't have a set time in my schedule for Facebook or Pinterest, an hour or more could go by, and I'll find I've not accomplished anything. Not only that, but I'm not better off, certainly not happier, for having spent that time on Facebook! A lot of crafters I've met complain that they spend more time on Pinterest pinning crafts than actually making things themselves! If they limited their time on Pinterest to 15 minutes for inspiration and scheduled their day properly, they would have *much* more free time to enjoy leisurely crafting. They would accomplish so much more!

64% Of Americans use Facebook. Facebook's primary purpose (or at least the reason most give for using it) is distraction and boredom relief. It's been shown to be addictive, compel us to compare our lives with others, and make people restless and uncomfortable. It also gives rise to cyberbullying, even among adults. Social media glamorizes drug and alcohol use and makes us unhappy. Political posts make us feel uncomfortable. People are less productive when one of the tabs open on their browser is a social media site. Sites like Facebook and Twitter are continually sending us notifications saying "Look at me!", distracting our attention from other, more worthy activities. Scheduling and Limiting your time on social media sites will help to curb the adverse effects associated with lingering on them.

What if I told you that you were probably doing something even worse for your productivity than spending hours on social media? What if I told you that this activity shuts down the thinking part of your brain, much like when you are asleep. What if I said that the average American spends 34 hours per week doing this one activity? Can you guess what it is?

It's watching television.

A recent study showed that the world's wealthiest people spend on average less than 1 hour per day watching TV, including movies and YouTube videos. Is television so bad for you? The rich will tell you that watching television is not only a waste of time but a distraction from your dreams and goals. It robs you of time you could spend to achieve your goals, time with your family, or out in nature. Television is full of unrealistic expectations, over done and airbrushed celebrities, and results in feelings of inadequacy as a result of watching. Remember that tidbit that social media is distracting and causing you to lose focus? Well, TV does the same thing, reducing your productivity significantly - so much for "multi-tasking"!

News has always been biased. The nature of bias is to convince you of a particular opinion. Once-independent and trustworthy news sources are being purchased en mass by large media conglomerates, and their content is changing to reflect the biases of the moguls that now own them. The Huffington Post, Vice Media, The Onion and even National Geographic have all changed their disposition considerably since being purchased by large media-centric corporations. Keep in mind that the word "bias" is not inherently bad. However, if you have a certain viewpoint, and you consume news that is representative only of *that* view, you may be missing out on part of the truth.

There is a saying that there are three sides to every story: his side, her side, and the truth. This can be said about nearly everything. One country's viewpoint, another country's viewpoint, and the truth. The right-wing opinion of this candidate, the left-wing opinion and the truth. Your opinion is yours, but you may find more balance and clarity if you formulate that opinion based upon multiple sources (and opinions) of information.

Television is overwhelmingly negative, with scarcely any redeeming messages, and the news only serves to desensitize us to the horrors of the world. The news is filled with reports of the most horrific events, the very worst of society. And these reports are sensationalized in such a way that they are nearly glorified. These stories are disproportionate to every day life, and often fail to share the good in society. If there are reports of good things and positive events, they are a token gesture compared to all the unspeakable acts that are displayed. Good and evil do not receive equal air time on the news! Is this the "information" you're seeking? In Chapter 13, I talk more about the news and politics, but for now allow me to caution you regarding the benefit of all the "news" you're consuming.

I probably don't need to convince you that watching television (and playing video games) is an unproductive way to spend your time. The truth is that it's not so bad if you want to schedule that favorite show into your calendar and get your "fix". My advice is to be aware of *how* you spend your time so that you can make a conscious choice about your screen time. Hold yourself accountable, and keep track of how much time you're spending. I guarantee that those lost hours watching television or playing video games can be put to better use! Just to be real - I spend about 1 hour per week watching television, and attend the occasional film. I also allow myself a small amount of time for crafts, games and social media.

I will make one caveat here - if you are playing video games and watch television with your children - especially older kids and teens, as a way of bonding, keep at it (in moderation). There is significant value in meeting teens *where they are*. I have done this in the past, and it was always an excellent opportunity to have those tougher conversations on their level. My daughter still calls home to thank me for those days we spent playing Second Life® or Minecraft together. It was valuable time spent!

Keeping your leisure screen time to a minimum shows your children that moderating their own time is valuable. The rich who limit or eliminate their game/television time will instead spend the leisure time they have scheduled on hobbies and spending time with their family. They play games, have family meetings and vacations, garden together and care for their homes together. I home educate, so a lot of my extra time is spent building giant Lego cities, crafting with my daughters and playing board games with them. At the end of the day, I'm much happier knowing that my children are certain of my love for them - because I spent my valuable time with them instead of glued to a screen. I don't want them to have childhood memories of the back of my head!

Build the habit

In order to implement a schedule in your life, simply start by making a list of all the things you'd like to schedule into your day. Note how often you want to do it, and how much time you feel the task will take. Next, make a rough draft schedule for each day of the week, adding your tasks in. Make sure you leave plenty of "margin" or space in your day that is unscheduled. This way, you have room to finish tasks that take longer than you planned and extra time to spend on unexpected events like receiving phone calls, family needs, and so forth. Practice your schedule over the next week, making notes and changes as you go. Be flexible.

Day 8: Declutter It All

It was an immense, black, Gothic candle stand. We kept it for several years after Mam's death because she was a classy woman who's influence was profoundly felt in my husband's family. The two families were tight-knit, and this woman was a well-respected matriarch. After her passing, her daughter had the duty of going through her belongings and determining what would be kept by the family, donated, or thrown away. What a challenging undertaking! The candle stand was a gift to Danger because of his close relationship with their family. It sat on our kitchen island for years, gathering dust. With the stand, my mother-in-law had generously added a large vanilla candle that fit in it perfectly, at the time we received it. Unfortunately, I wasn't a big fan of vanilla and with small children in the house, we rarely lit candles. Because the style of the candle stand didn't match the way we'd chosen to decorate our home, and we never burned the candle, it sat unused for years, but not discarded because it had come from this wonderful family. During the process of de-cluttering, I was able to offer it to my mother-in-law, who gladly accepted it. It was a relief to us to have it taken, but also, a joy to see that it was cherished by someone who knew Mam and the amazing woman that she was.

"Clutter is not just physical stuff.
It's old ideas, toxic relationships, and bad habits.
Clutter is anything that does not support your better self."
- Eleanor Brownn

The proverb "A place for everything and everything in its place." Has been attributed to Samuel Smiles, Mrs. Isabella Beaton, and Benjamin Franklin. It was well in use during the 18th century, and it's as apropos now as it was then.

Our personal space is a direct reflection of our thoughts and feelings on the inside. Clutter can represent a hesitance to commit, a procrastination problem, or simply our putting off difficult decision making. Clutter can also be our comfort. You can become accustomed to your clutter, and even the discontentment that it creates.

Physical clutter competes for your attention, making you less productive. It also overloads your senses and contributes to stress. Women often feel overwhelmed with their belongings, and worse, our children are feeling this as well. When children have too many objects, they are unable to keep their space neat and tidy and have difficulty determining where things should go.

Many of us have seen the beautiful images of perfect homes on Pinterest. It's not hard to spend an hour pinning images of dream homes, complete with vast libraries and beautiful meditation spaces. What you don't notice on first look is that most of the pictures you see of beautiful, perfect homes are minimalistic. Images of office spaces are not only neat and tidy, but devoid of paper clutter, unfinished projects or unpaid bills. The dining rooms of our ideal homes have clean, freshly painted walls and minimalist artwork, not children's drawings hastily taped to walls that haven't been cleaned since 1992.

Everyone enjoys a clean, neat, open space, so why don't we make an effort to create that space in *our* homes? I've admitted to having let go of three truckloads of clutter just this year. While I initially felt quite optimistic regarding this transition and work, more recently I'm feeling the pull to let go of even more. For myself, minimalism is a goal to aspire to, and quickly. I am motivated to continue, having seen the benefits apparent to myself and every other member of our family, not to mention how much better our home looks and feels!

Letting go of so much taught me that I am surrounded by objects that have no meaning for me. These things that I've acquired paint a representation of who I am and what I enjoy. Oddly, many of the things I let go of had no personal connection to me, and I'd never used them. For example, one drawer in my kitchen was so stuffed with cookie cutters, whisks and other utensils that I could hardly find what I needed when digging through it. After clearing out that drawer I discovered that over half of the objects inside were never even used, or they were in desperate need of replacing. I found myself awed at how much I'd accumulated that I didn't actually use.

During my de-cluttering I ask myself the following simple question: Do I love this or use this? If the answer is "no", then the object has to go! It's that simple! I realized that I was holding onto gifts that made me feel guilty when I thought of throwing them away or donating them. I also had clothing that didn't fit, or I didn't like, and shoes that hurt my feet when I wore them. I had kitchen appliances, purchased but rarely used because they were too complicated, and a ton of craft supplies that I'd never gotten around to using and was saving for rainy days.

There are no rainy days. Use it and love it, or let it go!

Children accumulate just like adults do, and it's our job to help our kids learn to de-clutter and let things go. We have a de-clutter party, and have a box for "donate" and another for trash. Children are naturally generous and are happy to donate unused or unloved toys. Broken toys are sometimes held onto for sentimental reasons, but should be eliminated if they're no longer functioning, sharp or dangerous, or if they don't align with your family's desires for your children (screen time restrictions, natural materials, anything that doesn't fit with your parenting goals, etc.).

We're in a fast-paced society. From every direction we're bombarded with advertising encouraging us to have what we want NOW, and "Don't wait, there's more!" The problem with this is that we end up with homes full of things we don't love and never use. We give gifts that aren't appreciated and then we make the recipient feel guilty if they don't like what we've given. We've become more withdrawn and anti-social, and we don't even know the recipients of our gifts well enough to get them something personal and appreciated. It's no wonder our children are falling into an attitude of entitlement and unappreciation.

Before giving a gift, ask the person what they need or want.

Observe whether their style is ostentatious or conservative. Make notes throughout the year as to the things they enjoy, have an interest in, or need. When it comes to children, ask their parents what kinds of items they prefer their children play with, and what things are off limits. Many parents prefer all-natural toys made from wood, hemp or cotton instead of plastic toys. Gifts that require batteries can add an extra complication and expense. Toys made in other countries run the risk of not conforming to the safety standards of your country. Some children have allergies or disorders that would cause them to be averse to some products, so it's doubly important to ask parent's for advice before making a purchase. In essence, make certain you give gifts that are relevant, thoughtful and will be appreciated.

Whenever possible, give memories instead of presents. Transition your children to going on adventures instead of opening gifts. Our family has enjoyed trips to the aquarium or zoo, skiing and even indoor skydiving instead of presents during birthdays. Older children that are out of the house should be able to provide for themselves, and we find it rewarding as a family to encourage continued memory-making with these older members of our family. We try to give tickets for events, ski/snowboarding lift tickets or passes to theme parks, zoos, and other venues. When grandparent's babysit, we often give them movie tickets in appreciation.

Like many other large endeavors, it's a good idea to set goals when you begin the process of de-cluttering. Some have found it helpful to set goals regarding how much they hope to let go of, and others have set goals that represent how much of each item they feel they need. I've seen some people limit their amount of clothing to 33 items, and others turn their hangers around and then put them straight after wearing something, enabling them to see what articles they never wore during the course of one year. Do what works best for you! I am constantly reminding myself to let go of anything I do not love. It is the most profound piece of advice for creating my space that I've encountered.

- Pick up an object and ask yourself if you love it or use it.
- If you don't love it, but you use it, ask yourself if you can replace it with something you *do* love.
- If you're unable to replace it at this time, determine where the object's home should be and put it there.
- If you don't love it or use it, let it go.
- If you don't use it, but you love it, ask yourself why you're keeping it and where its home should be.
- If it has a home and it's important to you, put it away.
- If you find that you don't have a home for the object, you don't use it and you're only keeping it out of obligation, let it go.

Yes, even family heirlooms. You see, heirlooms are simply objects that one person bought or made once upon a time. That person may or may not have loved that item, or even used it, but it stayed in the family for one reason or another. If you do not love it, and especially if you don't use it, you are under no obligation to that person to keep it. By all means, offer it to your family, take a photograph of it to save, but you do not need to keep any material object to be happy, healthy and whole.

Build the Habit

Begin the process of letting go of objects that no longer serve you and your family. You deserve to surround yourself with items that you love and use and have meaning for you. Let the rest go.

Day 9: Your Inner Circle

The three of us stood in the kitchen, trying to make sense of the online recipe Ruth had found for tamales. None of us had ever made them, but we were determined that our tamalada would be a success, and each of our families would have fresh tamales to eat for the next few days. Just as I was figuring out that we needed more lard so our cornmeal wouldn't be so dry, Kayla pulled me in for an awkward photo. I only say awkward because I'm 4'9" and she's 6'1." Even with her ducking and my standing on tip-toes, the picture looked incredibly silly. Despite our differences (physical, cultural, and religious), the three of us worked together to take over Ruth's dining table and create several dozen delicious tamales.

"Your friends should motivate and inspire you.
Your circle should be well-rounded and supportive.
Keep it tight. Quality over quantity, always."
- Unknown

"When the character of a man

Is not clear to you, look at
His friends."
- Japanese Proverb

"You are the average of the five people you spend the most time with"
- Jim Rohn

Your income, your mindset, and your emotional health are all impacted by the people around you. Studies show that your income will be the average of the salaries of your five closest friends. The people you spend the most time with affect nearly everything in your life. Spending time with successful people challenges you to become more successful. Happy people encourage those around them to be happier, and healthy people do the same. If you're not as confident as you'd like, spend time with confident people and watch your confidence soar! Are you trying to lose weight and become fit? Spending time with active people who make time for exercise will encourage you to become physically fit yourself.

Imagine you're 15 years old, and your mom just sat you down at the table to have "the talk." No, not **that** talk, the *friends* talk. Some of your friends are dragging you down. You know the ones. These are the people who discourage you, steal your dreams and drown you in their problems.

I'm talking about the empathizers, the realists, and the negative Nancies.

Empathizers are the people in your life that explode with

sympathy for anything they perceive as negative. These people want you to know how much they care about you, and they do so by voicing their concern on a regular basis. They aren't even aware that they're negative, because to them, they are only expressing care and concern. If you were to begin a conversation with "We got a flat tire today...", their response is inevitably to interrupt with something like "OMG! That's just terrible!" Unfortunately, because they are too busy focusing on something to empathize with, they miss the rest of the conversation.

Because these people mean well, it's important not to hurt their feelings or accuse them of being intentionally negative. Instead, you can take the approach of beginning any conversation with them in a positive fashion. Instead of starting with the flat tire, I say "We had a wonderful unexpected stop today near a field of sunflowers. Then we took pictures and sang songs. It was the best flat tire we've ever had!" By starting with the positive portion of the message, and focusing on it, our empathizer has no need to express concern. You can enjoy a conversation with them free from negativity.

The realists are always there to calm down anyone who's too excited about something that isn't a worthwhile endeavor. They're quick to let you know not to "quit your day job" and to remind us that our dreams are too big/aspirational/unrealistic. They discourage anything risky and put down any ideas that are too far from the societal norm. They're the ones who think that because someone else is already doing something, it's not worth us attempting our version. The problem is, these people are expressing lack of faith in our abilities, blatant distrust, and disrespect for us. With their constant barrage of negativity and putting down of our ideas, they are sending up an enormous red flag that says "I don't think you can do it!" and it *hurts*.

While they have been some of the toughest conversational moments I've ever had, I directly confronted these people. I ask them why they don't have faith in me. I question why they shoot down every idea I've had. Then, I ask them what exactly is it that they fear? When it got right down to it, most of the time they were concerned that my potential failure could somehow affect them or their lifestyle. They were worried about how they might look if I failed or made a fool out of myself. In nearly every encounter with a person like this that I've had, these people really wanted some continuity and took comfort in the norm. They didn't want my dreams to change their version of reality, or to force them to question their lifestyle or achievements. Many people resist change, but when it means that I lose support for my dreams, I have to confront that person and let them know how it feels. I'm happy to answer questions and alleviate concerns. However, if they can't be positive, I'll just reduce my contact with that person and avoid talking to them about my plans in the future.

The third type of negative person is the most challenging. Negative Nancy will rain on your parade every time. Her favorite topic of conversation is her horrible life, and she can't wait to share it with you. Her car broke down…again. Her kids are awful and don't respect her. She's always broke, always complaining and always unloading onto you. Every time you have a conversation with this person, it leaves you feeling drained and down. There is no upside, no light at the end of the tunnel. This person is simply on another wavelength from you. They are not able to see the joy in their lives, much less yours.

This person can do with a good dose of gratitude! Start by asking "Nancy" what is going *well* in her life. Ask her about the beautiful things she's seen this week, or what her favorite flower is. Always try to turn the conversation around to something happy. Unhappy people are uncomfortable around happy people - often, they're just not ready to be happy. Sometimes you just have to come out and say that "I'm building a beautiful life of joy, and I'd really like you to participate. If you are able to do so, then great - let's talk about something happier. If not, then please give me a call when you're feeling up to it!"

Another tip: If at any time during a conversation, someone is hyperbolic, using words like "always" or "never", when they clearly mean something else like "often" or "sometimes," correct them immediately. Teenagers are especially prone to this way of speaking, and it's unfortunately fatalistic, damaging, and negative. Gently correcting them "I believe you mean that *many* of your friends have new iPhones. I know Jamie doesn't have one, and neither does Carl, but I can understand your interest in them, and frustration over not getting one."

Your closest friends influence the way you think. You typically surround yourself with people who have similar attitudes regarding politics, religion, level of ambition, style of dress and even home decor. The opinion your friends hold regarding your achievements or even new things you learn or discover will have an impact on whether or not you continue those pursuits. It is imperative that you surround yourself with positive, upbeat, energetic DOERS. If the people that are closest to you have that much influence, then you'll want them to be the very best you can find. How then, do you reach out to people who will benefit you?

First, we have to get over ourselves. We've got to stop worrying about not being good enough. You are divine! You deserve to have the life you want, and that starts inside. Let go of those negative feelings that bubble up and tell you that you don't deserve to have wealthy, fit, confident and successful friends. Just let that go! You deserve those friends, you can have those friends, and you will have those friends! Not only that, you deserve to be wealthy, fit, to feel confident and successful too - often having friends that represent those qualities will help to inspire you to achieve or believe them as well.

How do you find people who reflect your personal dreams and goals? You reach out to the kind of people **you** would be able to call mentors. If you've ever been inside someone's beautiful home and thought "I wish my home looked this beautiful!" Give that person a call, and invite them to coffee. Then, talk to them about their home. Compliment their success in creating that beautiful haven, then ask them about their process for achieving it. We all love to be complimented, and asking about things we're passionate about is extremely flattering. You can use the same process for someone who is fitter than you, a mom who's parenting you admire, etc. Just ask them about their journey and how they got to where they are! That's how it starts; then you build a friendship the same as any other - with concern, conversation, and shenanigans.

Join local groups for activities you're hoping to learn or are interested in, and read books or listen to podcasts by successful people in industries you want to learn more about. Meetup.com is an excellent site for finding local people with common interests.

Your inner circle of friends is vitally important, but so is your outer circle. On social media, I recommend unfollowing anyone who is regularly negative, crude or bullying. I would also unfollow people who are overly political or who seem angry with everything. When you're focusing on building a life of joy and abundance, you have to cut off those things that bring you down or continually try to pull you back to the mediocre.

Notice that I recommended "unfollowing" as opposed to unfriending on social media. I'm not advocating that you call Uncle Joe up and tell him that you're never speaking to him again because of his weird conspiracy theories. What I am saying, is that unlimited contact with people who illicit negativity constantly can be draining. There are a lot of people out there who are mired in misery. You don't have to be one of them, and you don't have to listen to it or read about it either.

Build the Habit

Analyze your circle of friends. Take action to change the conversation when it turns negative, and let your inner circle know that you are transforming your life from one of negativity to one of joy. Focus on the positive, especially when talking to your empathizing friends, let your negative Nancy and "realist" friends know of your desires and ask them to support you in that endeavor. Seek out mentors and positive people to cultivate relationships with, and unfollow the downers on social media. Surround yourself with successful, ambitious DOERS, and watch your life transform!

Day 10: Relationships

It could have been much worse. In the end, it turned out to be a strange haircut indeed, but it wasn't a pixie cut. I did lose more than 8 inches of length, and the hair in the back of my head was full of blunt layers, many far shorter than I had anticipated. The cosmetology instructor had come over and finished the pieces in the front, warning my daughter that if she'd cut the front of my hair that short, I would have killed them both. What she didn't know was that it didn't matter how strange my hair turned out in the end - I was there for my daughter, and nothing more. Kirsten was finishing the all-too-brief hair cutting portion of her cosmetology instruction at the community college in La Junta, Colorado and I had promised to show up and allow her to color and cut my hair. I ended up with two slightly different colors (split right down the center of my head), and hair short enough that I shed a few tears at its loss, and was baffled as to how I should style it for months. Nevertheless, my goal wasn't beauty, but a gift for Kirsten. I just wanted her to know that I supported her fully in her endeavor, and I would have let her shave it had that been a requirement for her certificate.

"Friendship is not a big thing,
It's a million little things."
- Unknown

"Be an encourager.
The world has plenty of critics already."
- Dave Willis

In the last chapter we discussed the importance of designing your inner circle to uplift and encourage you. Fortifying friendships and maintaining close relationships is key to keeping your inner circle well-fed with your love and appreciation. When you look at the relationships you have in your life, some close and some distant, you can see that not only does your level of care and attention vary, but the reciprocation and intensity of feelings changes from person to person. You may have relationships that are intimate and close (our spouse, parents, children) and those that are quite distant (cashier, waitress, customer service). In each of these relationships, you can do small things and large that will leave lasting good impressions. It's easier than you think to make people feel special and respected. Building trust and confidence can result in everything from a loving marriage to the lasting respect of your peers and better service or discounts from your favorite restaurant. Volumes could be written regarding how to build strong friendships, parent & child relationships, and marriages. Here are a few of my favorite techniques that have had a lasting impact on the cherished relationships in my life.

It is most important to make sure your spouse or partner is

cherished and made to feel special and loved on a daily
Relationships are hard work - don't let anyone tell you they're e
or that you can stop working at it after you leave the altar. There
is never an end to the appreciation you can give to your spouse for their presence in your life, and the myriad small things they do for your family throughout the day. People regularly ask me what to do when marriage becomes rocky. The one thing I say is that you need to be the partner you want before you can get the partner you desire.

Being an ideal partner is challenging, and perhaps too unrealistic for us to aspire to. Start small, and work your way up. Begin with gratitude, being thankful for your partner every single day. Take time to appreciate their presence in your life every morning, and every evening. By utilizing gratitude, your attitude toward your partner will change, and thoughts of resentment, critical judgments, and even small irritations will melt away.

Next, start practicing some of the actions you hope to see your partner emulate. Do you want them to be more spontaneous? Then *you* should practice spontaneity. Do you want them to appreciate all the little things that you do? Then *you* should be thanking them for all the small things that they do. Not only do you lead your children by example, but you lead the adults around you as well. Etiquette, charm and endearing moments of love are qualities that we emulate, especially after seeing them demonstrated by someone we hold in high esteem.

Friendships work similarly, but without the same degree of intimacy and dependency. If you can recall some of the nicest

nave done for you, some of the best compliments
of compassion, examples of heroism or class that
ou, then by all means assimilate those qualities into
tion to your actions in romantic relationships, you
e kind of friend you'd like to see in the people around you. Let go of the worry that you'll be taken advantage of - that worry is a fear based on relationships of poor choosing. Remember that you're formulating an inner circle of people that are going to challenge you to be a greater version of yourself. If the people in your life don't fit that bill, then we'll lovingly let them go and find others who will.

We move in and out of different social circles all the time. I urge you to become a better friend to the people in your life while respecting yourself enough to know when there are people in your circle that are only draining you of energy and joy. Begin spending more and more of your time with people who positively challenge you instead.

If I've learned anything about cultivating friendships, it's that you must speak and write to them with genuine love and appreciation. There is nothing classier than receiving a hand-written thank-you note in the mail after an evening well spent. I realize that Facebook, texts and emails have become quite commonplace, but I shirk them when it comes to communicating with my friends and family in meaningful ways. Buy yourself a lovely fountain pen, and sit down and write some letters to friends and relatives. I guarantee that the responses you'll receive (even if only online) will be well worth your time.

Take the time to know your friends and family well enough that you can get them meaningful gifts for their birthday and the holidays. It is so nice to open a gift and know that the person who gave it, knew them well enough to purchase something they would genuinely appreciate. Give something representative of their taste in attire, home decor, music, or reading material, without challenging their style and interests. If you can, keep a list of gift ideas throughout the year, to draw upon during the holidays. I keep such a list for each of my family members, and for a few close friends. When something is mentioned in conversation, or someone voices a wish or desire, I jot it down in my list for that person so that I can get them a related gift or hand make something appropriate. Whenever someone compliments food I've made, if it's something I can replicate easily and give as a gift, I do that as well.

When you're with friends, talk about *them* as much as possible. People are far more interested in themselves than they are in you. It's true of us all. The fact is that if you want to build friendships or romance, you should concentrate on building relationships. That means investing your time, your interest and your listening skills in them. It means asking them about what they're interested in, about their hobbies, their children, their dreams. There is no better way to build a friendship or a relationship than to show genuine interest in another person and *their* interests.

There are two occasions where even casual acquaintances will receive a visit and food from me. Can you guess them? They are births and funerals. I always make an easy-to-thaw oven-ready casserole for births. This way, the parents can toss the meal in the freezer, and pull it out and bake it in the days after the baby is born to ease the family's burden. Restaurant gift certificates, gift bags for siblings, and an offer to help around the house or care for a newborn so mother can rest are all appropriate and well-received new baby gifts (aside from what might be expected if you're invited to a shower).

In the event of a funeral, I always ask the family what they would like. They're often already inundated with food and flowers, and many have a fund set up for expenses or a charity they'd like to donate toward in lieu of flowers. I've learned from close friends who've experienced grief that it's important not to be afraid to speak to them about the situation, or to offer support even when we don't know what to say. Sometimes just being present is a gift, but know that in the weeks after family has gone home and it's time for life to settle back into a new "normal" - that's when your friend will need you the most. Don't be afraid to reach out during this time.

Being a good partner or friend comes down to using the empathy you have to relate with people in a meaningful way. I strive to treat my husband in a way that makes him feel loved and appreciated. I work to show my friends that I'm glad they're a part of my life, and I let them know at every opportunity. If you focus on the life you want, the friendships and the **love** you want in your life, and then work toward being that lover, that friend, to the people in your life, your circle will reflect that. The people in your life will rise to the occasion, and you'll attract people into your life that are echoes of your actions.

You attract people who are like you. Your friends are more

like you than different, and there's a reason for that - leaving your comfort zone is challenging. Because you enjoy who you are, and are comfortable with your style and actions, you'll be more comfortable with others who are similar. **If you're constantly striving to be a better friend, a better lover, a better son or daughter, the people in your life will evolve to meet your new standard for yourself, or they will step aside, so the new people you are attracting have room to bless you.**

As a child, my best friend was Steffani. She was wonderful, and everything that I wasn't. She was blond, tall and thin and came from a middle-class family. I was short, my hair was darkening on an almost daily basis and I came from a poor family. I adored her, and spent as much time as possible at her home enjoying her company, and that of her family. We shared interests in science fiction films, super star crushes like Rutger Hauer and Will Wheaton and we talked long into the night about the probability that we were really aliens, expecting a rescuing mother ship any day. As we aged, we grew apart. She was growing and becoming wiser at a faster pace than I. It all came to a head during her non-traditional wedding, wherein it was clear that not only were our lifestyles different, but our religions were as well. In one of the most tragic moves of my life, I thrust her away, because her beliefs were different, her lifestyle confused me and I didn't see her as belonging in my life anymore. I regretted my decision for years. I sent letters of apology to old addresses, always having them returned to me. I was incredibly grateful when I was able to reconnect with her on Facebook. She is still the wise, beautiful woman that I remember, and although we don't share the closeness that we had as schoolgirls, and may never again, I am thankful to have had the opportunity to let her know how much she meant to me.

Keep in mind that as you grow to be a better version of yourself, there may be those in your life who say or do things they may regret later. Your gracious understanding will go a long way toward preserving friendships, even as you seek to improve your relationships and attract new people into your life. When you observe a friend in a period of growth, expressing your genuine interest and curiosity, without judgment, can be one of the best gifts you can offer. When you're growing into your divine nature, you are still the person you were yesterday - only better.

Build the habit

Relationships are built on small things that add up to big feelings. Do something small every day to cultivate the relationships you want to flourish. Practice genuine appreciation daily. Build or grow a relationship by reaching out and talking with someone regarding what interests *them*. Show your children that you appreciate them, and regularly thank them for their contribution to the family. Practice granting grace to friends and loved ones who are working to change their life for the better, and give them the freedom to do so in the way that serves them best.

Mindset
changes

Ten mindset changes to consider on your path to joy.

"When you are joyful, when you say yes to life and
And have fun and project positivity all around you,
You become a sun in the center of every constellation,
And people want to be near you."
- Shannon L. Alder

Day 11: Poverty to Abundance

I opened the envelope and showed Danger the contents. In a very short amount of time, I had not only saved enough money for the tickets to Burning Man (an 8-day camping art festival in the Nevada desert) but most of the travel and other expenses for the trip. He was surprised at my willpower and ability to save so much in such a short period. I explained that it wasn't willpower, but motivation. I had wanted to experience this gathering for years, and I kept imagining standing in the shadow of 50-foot art projects and experiencing the gifting community at the event. Those images were so exciting and made me feel so good, that I relished putting money inside that envelope. Anytime I sold something or received any funds; I put as much as possible in that envelope. Attending the event with friends, watching the explosions and fireworks as the man burned, and the emotional experience of the temple all served to fuel the pride I had in saving my money for the event. I got to cross an item off my bucket list to boot!

"Success, just like poverty, is a state of mind.

You can become successful instantly
With a simple decision and commitment.
Long lasting and pronounced success
Comes to those who renew their commitment
To a mindset of abundance
Every minute, hour, and day.
- Bryant H. McGill

In order to transform your financial situation, it is imperative that you change how you view wealth. I grew up in a low-income family. We were practically destitute while my mother attended college and my father worked as a woodworker for a 5-star resort hotel. His salary barely made ends meet, and we were always concerned that we wouldn't be able to afford school supplies, clothes, and even food. I have memories of thrift stores, food pantries and government-issued black and white generic cheese.

It was this childhood experience that fostered in me a drive for success. Since I was required to earn my way at a young age, and raise money for most non-necessities myself, I have always been keen to work hard and strive for financial freedom. I've never owned a credit card, have a natural tendency to save money and practice delayed gratification often.

However, when I moved out and began experiencing adulthood and all the financial responsibility that entails, I learned something interesting about my parents. They feel that wealth is evil. We endured all of their economic struggle, all the years of stress and strain due to lack. I learned that my parents would have felt guilty making enough money to spare us all of that pain. They've often judged wealthy celebrities harshly, successful business owners especially so.

While I adore my parents and feel that they've done the best they were able to at the time, I disagree with their feelings regarding wealth and abundance. I don't understand the opinion many of my friends have, that there isn't enough money to go around, or that only a limited few can achieve great wealth. I've seen many people rise to wealth from nothing because they practiced *habits* that nearly guaranteed their eventual success. The rich in every country are in the highest tax brackets and give the most to charity. Rich people create jobs and invent things that make our lives better. Risk-taking entrepreneurs have taken us from an agrarian society into the space age. Even when they spend money on opulence, it creates many jobs, and they pay huge property taxes and maintenance fees which benefit the poor.

Hard work only gets you so far when it comes to achieving wealth. You also have to change your attitude toward money and abundance. If you believe that there isn't enough, or that you aren't deserving, or that somehow only a chosen few will succeed, then your efforts will be in vain. Believing there is enough wealth for everyone, that you are deserving of financial freedom, and feeling truly happy for others' success is key to achieving prosperity yourself.

I believe that my poverty as a child has given me the impetus to work hard and achieve more as an adult. Still, many others learn from their parent's habits of lack. They complain incessantly about money - or the lack thereof. They berate a restaurant because of their prices; they whine because they can't afford to take their family to the movies; or they put people down for making purchases that they can't afford themselves.

My husband and I have met hundreds of people over the years that we hoped we could be friends with. The poverty mindset is one of the first things we pick up on, and it's one of the biggest barriers to meaningful friendships that we have encountered. Having an abundance mindset is one of the most fundamental parts of my paradigm. It is a foundation for our financial outlook, and it drives nearly all of our financial decisions. Because of that, we cannot afford to attract people into our circle that have a poverty mindset. In a world conditioned to embracing lack, feeding on negative commentary and continual "poor me" Facebook posts; those people with an abundance mindset not only stand out, they rise to the top.

Tony Robbins says that "People are rewarded in public for what they practice for years in private." Your financial mindset can either be a crutch for poverty or a catalyst toward wealth. Letting go of negative views regarding money is the first step in transforming your outlook from one of poverty to one of abundance. Begin telling yourself that you are deserving of wealth, that there is an infinite supply of money for you to tap into, and that you have the ability to achieve financial success.

"I am deserving of wealth."
"There is an infinite supply of money for me to tap into at any time."
"I have all the support and creativity I need to achieve financial

success."

"There are always open doors of opportunity and prosperity in my life."

Next, begin practicing the habits that lead to wealth. Develop the habit of delayed gratification. Take time to consider every purchase in the light of whether or not it is in line with wealth creation. My husband and I have often forgone going out to dinner and put the money we would have spent into savings, purchased silver or other metals or added it to our business or investment capital. From the time they are walking, our children are taught to "pay themselves first" by putting 1/3 of their allowance into an account for future investments.

Debt is one of the most effective deterrents to wealth, and yet it is consistently praised in the media and encouraged by society. As far as financial mistakes go, buying a car with a payment, rent-to-own furniture, and payday loan services are surely some of the worst you can make. I find these business models morally abhorrent, because they take advantage of the poor, encourage spending without the income necessary to buy those items, and they overcharge the very people who would have the most to gain from delaying their purchases. We advise our children to have an emergency fund set up before leaving home, and my husband and I always have at least six months of living expenses set aside, plus more for emergencies like car and home repairs. Even a very small amount put away every month leads to quite a bit over time.

$5 per week would net you $260 at the end of the year. $10 per week, $520.

And just $25 per week would give you $1300 after a year of saving.

Don't allow yourself to think that you're unable to save money. If you purchase any coffee (that you don't have to brew yourself), go out to eat, buy food with empty calories, you can cut something. Better yet, invest in yourself and start a business or learn a valuable new skill. Use a portion of this money for your savings. If you keep track of your spending as Dave Ramsey recommends, you'll find money you are spending that is unnecessary, or doesn't fit in the paradigm of wealth creation or goal achievement. Yes, this means living on less than your income. If there isn't enough money at the end of the month, you have two choices - live on less or earn more. You cannot save your way to wealth, but you can save your way to security, and use your natural skills and talents to make extra money for investments.

Live within your means. Remind yourself that your abundance mindset is leading you on a path toward wealth - not a path of greater spending. Don't fool yourself into a false mindset wherein you're spending money you don't have or can't afford to lose, on projects that won't have a direct financial return. You could be setting yourself up for financial ruin. Most lottery winners are so unprepared for their wealth, with no idea of how to manage it or maintain it, that they become broke (or grossly indebted) shorty after receiving it. We have a culture of anti-wealth sentiment, pressure to consume and a blatant attack on financial education. However, we can segregate ourselves from the masses through self-education, so that our families thrive and *build* wealth instead of shunning it.

Work to constantly improve your relationship with, and knowledge of, money. Learn financial language, educate yourself about the stock market and different kinds of investments. Research real estate investing with no money down. Read everything you can by Dave Ramsey and Robert & Kim Kiyosaki. Join an investment meetup near you and let them know you're there to learn.

Read about making passive income online. I recommend starting at WarriorForum.com. The people there are welcoming to new learners, and the older posts are a wealth of information on making an income online. **Never** pay for information on how to make money online. You can learn everything you need to know for free! Watch videos, join forums or Facebook groups. Network and ask questions.

Wealthy people are constantly improving themselves and are driven to succeed in every area of their life, not just in their pocketbooks. They work hard on their relationships, their fitness level, their spiritual journey, and they are continually working on self-improvement. These people are not afraid to admit that they are growing or working to learn something new. Many will be the first to tell you that they are *not* experts. Nearly every single one has at least one mentor or coach or has had one or more in the past.

Isaac Newton encouraged us to "Stand on the shoulders of giants". Whatever you want to do, someone has written a book on that subject (and likely many have). Read constantly. I read over an hour a day, and I usually have three books going at once, all non-fiction. I rarely read fiction or watch television because I find that I don't have time for it. I'm too busy improving myself, too busy learning. Human knowledge is vast and constantly evolving. Take advantage of it, and watch your prospects grow!

One of my girlfriends recently told me that I was the richest person she knew. I don't live in a mansion, and I don't own any $1,000 purses. It wasn't my material possessions or the size of my home, but my attitude toward it all that impacted her. When you implement small changes which, over the course of time, change your inward beliefs toward wealth and abundance, your outer life reflects those changes. It's like washing the windows on the outside of your home and realizing that it's the inside of the glass that is dirty. Your mindset can shift, giving you a broader, more positive viewpoint if you let it.

Change your mind

Today, begin telling yourself that you are worthy of wealth. Start practicing appreciation for the abundance other people are experiencing. Notice their cars, their clothing, their purchases in the grocery line, and be genuinely happy for them. Begin practicing delayed gratification, and weighing your purchases. Give yourself permission to say no, to save instead of spend, and to wait to make a purchase. Get in the habit of spending time learning about wealth and how you can achieve it.

Day 12: Stress to Mindfulness

I sat quietly meditating, listening to the guide from an app on my phone via headphones. The house was quiet, me being the only one awake. The meditation was pleasant, and the guide's voice was calm and unhurried. I felt completely at peace and knew that it was the perfect beginning to a great day. I was enjoying this relaxing moment when I felt two arms; then four encircle me. I was held in place for about 30 seconds by two of my children while I continued to finish the meditation. They neither spoke or moved, just hugged me until I finished the session. Afterward, I opened my eyes to find my nine and seven-year-old girls, grinning and ready for breakfast.

> "The mind can go in a thousand directions,
> but on this beautiful path, I walk in peace.
> With each step, the wind blows.
> With each step, a flower blooms."
> - Thích Nhất Hạnh

Stress and the negative health repercussions from it are becoming more and more common. An analysis published in the Journal of Applied Social Psychology in 2012 detailed how stress has been shown to have increased by 18% for women and 25% for men since 1983. The report also revealed increasingly greater stress for those who have lower incomes and less education. The experts who completed the study weren't surprised by the results, commenting that compared to the early 1980's, today "economic pressures are greater, it's harder to turn off information, and it's harder to buffer ourselves from the world."

Our brain works hard to fight stress and situations that it deems detrimental to our health and well-being. Our amygdala acts as a kind of security guard, rising to protect us in dangerous situations. It is this mental "security guard" that asks "What's going on here?" when you hear a crash from the kitchen and run to investigate. It is this same part of your brain that perks up when you hear a sound at night and don't know what's lurking in the darkness. If you've ever experienced the fight or flight response, it is your amygdala once again, doing what it does best to protect us from danger.

While our amygdala serves an important purpose, there are many times when you want your amygdala just to chill out and relax! The problem is that it's beating the reasoning parts of your brain to understand what is happening, and taking control. In order to calm down your amygdala and react more reasonably to situations, you have to breathe and practice the habit of calming your mind *before* you act.

Mindfulness is the simple act of being aware of what is going on around you. It's the practice of recognizing the facts of your environment, without passing judgment. In order to build your mindfulness "muscle", you start by becoming more aware of the simple, the silent and the situation. I'm going to give you some specific mindfulness practices later in the book, but for now, let's talk about the one thing you can do every day that will guarantee not only a dramatic reduction in your stress level but also give you a jump start on your mindfulness practice.

You may have already guessed that I'm talking about meditation. There are three main forms of meditation, guided, focused and unfocused. During guided meditation, you would listen to someone take you on a mental journey. There are free guided meditations on YouTube if you'd like to explore this method. Guided meditation is helpful for beginners, because the guides help you to redirect your thoughts to the present moment, and it requires less discipline to get into a state of relaxation. Many advanced meditators still use the guided method because it's a wonderful way to explore a particular concept (like peace, love, or patience) while meditating. It's comforting to have a guide who can continually bring your thoughts back to focus on the subject when your mind wanders. It is a simple form of meditation, but not less effective than any other, which is why it's extremely popular.

Focused meditation is the next step up. Using this method, practitioners will focus on something in order to deter wayward thoughts. During their meditation, they would gently redirect their thoughts to the focus. A focus could be a sound like the breath or a mantra like "OM", an image or a phrase from scripture or even a way of thinking. Some practitioners, for example, might focus on healing an illness, being more compassionate of other drivers on the road, or on how they might be more peaceful parents. Any time the mind wanders from the focus, you gently bring your thoughts back in line. There's no stress or frustration in this action - even if it occurs many times throughout the session. The brain benefit is achieved in the times that you are in focus, and the "muscle building" happens when you guide your wayward, busy thoughts back to it - both are valuable.

Unfocused meditation is one of the most interesting and introspective of practices. During an unfocused meditation practice, a person simply sits and observes their thoughts. They watch as their mind races from idea to idea, taking an interest, but not engaging any of the thoughts, worries or anxieties. During this practice, the participant might also make a point to observe the stillness between thoughts as well. It is in this stillness that you find the most peace and comfort, and it is in the observance of your thoughts without interacting with them or giving them energy or fuel, that you grow. During this kind of meditation session, the following thought process may take place:

> "I see I'm worried about money." - pushes the thought away, as if it is a balloon, and enjoys the quiet peace between thoughts.
> "I see that I am remembering my daughter laughing earlier today." - sends the thought away, enjoys the peace between.
> "I see that I can hear the music from a car driving by." - sends the thought away, enjoys the peace between.

Repeat this process until the end of the session.

Mindfulness can also be found via prayer, taking a walk, or a relaxing bath. It is also the act of putting ourselves wholly into a menial task like sweeping, cleaning dishes, or folding laundry. Mindfulness is simply taking care of *you* while slowing down and bringing your mind to a pure state of just *being*. You must fill your cup before you can serve others. In order to fully give yourself to a project, your spouse, your family, or your career, you have to ground and recover and fill your spirit with the vital energy needed to cultivate patience, strength of will, and joy.

Our response to any given situation is what *really* effects the outcome. My husband often tells the story of how his home was burglarized in his early 20's. He was on vacation and returned home to discover that someone had backed a U-Haul into his driveway, loaded up all his possessions and disappeared. He lost everything he owned, including family heirlooms that had been entrusted to him. Like most people, his initial reactions were anger, disbelief, and distress. But after a short time, he felt a weight lifted and was encouraged to live more minimally. Since then, he has lived without a strong attachment to material goods.

It was his reaction that made the situation bearable. He filed a report with the police department and moved on. Because there was nothing he could do to change the situation, he simply let it go and moved on with his life. My husband could have reacted quite differently to that situation. He could have interrogated his neighbors, or hounded the police daily for weeks in hopes of finding the culprit. Instead, he took the attitude that the person who robbed him needed those things more than he did. Since the entire situation was beyond his control to change, he let it go and moved on with his life.

While I'm not sure I could have reacted the same way that he did, I do know that breeding discontentment, in any situation is inherently bad for us. Training ourselves to react in a non-stressful way, to ask ourselves "What would a Buddhist Monk do?", "What would my higher self do?" or "What would Jesus do?" really does help us to react in a better way to a given situation. By constantly reminding yourself of your ability to act peacefully and productively, you grow to take on that mindset and create the outcome you desire.

Have you ever watched a film and noticed a plot twist? Like when we discovered that Vader was Luke's father in Star Wars™. It was a surprise that changed how we viewed both Luke and Vader, and how we imagined Luke's future to be. When the unexpected happens in your life, you can choose to shout "Plot twist!" and enjoy the experience of life's surprises with a bit of humor.

When you react poorly to a situation, you train your brain to enjoy the adrenaline rush, and the negative feelings like panic, anger, frustration, and rage. Every time you react this way, you fuel an addiction in your brain. When you visualize acting calmly in these situations, you retrain your brain to allow rational thought to take over, and you end the cycle of yelling, violence, panic and stress that so often accompanies day-to-day experiences. It takes years to perfect, and most of us can't transform our reactions overnight. You can work toward a better self one day at a time - one event at a time. Throughout this process, it is important to be gentle with yourself; recognizing mistakes without punishing yourself for them. You are enough just the way you are!

Change your mind

Explore meditation, prayer, and nature. Begin the practice of reacting calmly and peacefully to the world around you. Gently remind yourself of your goal to be more mindful. Refrain from passing judgment if your amygdala reacts before you can look at a situation with rationale or mindfulness. Trust the process.

DAY 13: CONFIRMATION BIAS TO MINDFUL AWARENESS

There has been a trend in negativity toward law enforcement in social media, and the news. In an effort to balance the inputs I have been receiving, I began following pro-law enforcement groups on Facebook and researching what departments were doing to curb corruption and violence. The balance has helped me to take on a healthier mindset toward police officers and eased my fears and concerns regarding the officers in my area. By seeking balance, and by educating myself outside of the bias I have been exposed to, I have been able to develop a healthier mindset toward modern law enforcement, and a genuine excitement for the future of the industry.

"Confirmation bias is the most effective way
To go on living a lie."
- Criss Jami

"We meet aliens every day who have
Something to give us. They come

In the form of people with different opinions."
- William Shatner

If everyday distractions like the constant "ping" of tweets, notifications, and texts are causing us added stress and strain, then how much more damaging to our peace of mind are politics and the news? You are constantly being marketed to, advertised to and bombarded with opinions on every facet of life. Your pocketbook, vote, opinion and your time are being competed for on a minute-by-minute basis by companies, politicians and organizations. No wonder we're struggling to reduce stress, maintain our marriages and keep our families together!

Often the first reaction I receive from someone when I tell them that I no longer watch the news is "But how do you get informed?" At that point I ask them, "What has being "informed" done for you?" "Can you name a news story you consumed in the last six months that actually made any real difference in the way you've lived your life?" Watching the news has become more and more irrelevant to the average person. In 2003 a landmark legal case sided on behalf of the news networks and the FCC's News Distortion Policy. This policy encourages news agencies to report the truth, stating that "rigging or slanting the news is a most heinous act against the public interest." While this policy is a strong recommendation for ethics in journalism, it is not law. A CNN anchor came out the same year, claiming that all news was for sale to the highest bidder. Other journalists report regularly that they were fired after reporting on something particularly damning to a corporation, political party or country that is funding their former employer. It is important that you research what you are seeing and reading, and that you obtain your news from varied sources to ensure that the information you are receiving is accurate as well as unbiased.

If the news isn't helping us to lead better lives, and if it can't entirely be trusted, can we at least say that it isn't harmful? Not exactly. Watching the news has been shown to trigger our limbic system, causing increased stress and feelings of fear and paranoia, and it can lead to desensitization. Watching the news makes you fearful, and in return you feel as though you *need* to watch more of it so you can be informed about all the things you need to be fearful of. Then you justify your time spent by telling yourself that you're able to talk to other people about what's going on in the world, and communicate your feelings of distrust, concern and worry about the future. In addition, you worry about being "right" and can't wait to express your opinion on social media, even going so far as to post things like "Unfriend me right now if you don't agree!" on Facebook.

How sad is it that we purposefully remove people from our lives because their opinions are different from our own! This is called confirmation bias, and the news contributes to it. Confirmation bias is our natural human tendency to search for information that confirms our already held judgments and beliefs. It's so uncomfortable for us to have our beliefs and opinions challenged that we continually seek out opportunities to confirm our opinions, and to fellowship with people who feel similarly to the way we do. Unfortunately, this doesn't help us grow, on the contrary, it contributes to racism, xenophobia, and ignorance.

How do you avoid confirmation bias? First, be aware that your natural tendency will be to confirm your already held beliefs. Be willing to accept that you can learn, or more importantly that you might be wrong about some things. Actively seek differing opinions, and invite friendships with people who are different from you. Instead of focusing on being right, focus on the process of learning and growing and sharing with others. Enjoy intellectual conversation without making it a debate. You can find another person's opinion interesting, *without* trying to change it. Ask questions!

We learn by exercising our ability to seek the truth. A scientist seeking to confirm an opinion will run an experiment to test a hypothesis, but his experiment runs the risk of bias if he doesn't also admit the opposite opinion may also be fact. You can benefit from this approach for *every* issue you are confronted with. By studying an opposing point of view, you are able to know whether your current opinion is valid or not. Your belief becomes stronger, not diluted with unsupported ideas. You can attain mindful balance and find the joy in knowing *all* the facts, instead of only those that support one side of an issue.

While it might be possible for someone to turn off the news occasionally to give their mind a break from the negativity, it's much harder to tune out politics. We enjoy our media-driven political circuses! The emotionally charged debates, campaign phone calls, and solicitous mail all add to our confirmation bias and give us conversational fodder for family gatherings. Politics make us feel like we're on a "team" for the betterment of humanity. It provides us with a feeling of participation and contribution to our country.

Politics also have a dark side. We can get so worked up in a fervor regarding our opinion that we have heated discussions that damage our relationships. We spend hours online reading about the problems of the world, and little time making positive changes in our communities. We rant and rave on Facebook, limiting our friendships to only those who share similar beliefs, and causing discomfort in our wake. Emotionally charged issues are our soapbox, and we're pushing our opinion upon everyone we meet.

The problem is that while this feeds our ego, our need to belong in a group, and our sense of patriotism, it doesn't make us feel happy. It also doesn't do any *real* good in the world. The hours we spend complaining about the things we disagree with, diminish the time that we could spend on the things that we love and wish to promote. Anger and self-righteousness are unhealthy emotions that damage relationships. It's not worth it.

I vote. I feel glad to vote, and I'm thankful for the women who fought so I could have that right. In order to vote responsibly, with adequate information on the topic, without pressure and without too much of my time being taken away from positive pursuits, I vote absentee. I vote from home so that I may take my time and research the issues and candidates. In addition, I limit my political intake or education until about a month prior to an election. I don't watch the news, debates, keynotes or addresses until just prior to an election. I actively seek both sides of an argument, and I look at the track records of the candidates instead of just listening to their words.

Using this method frees me to live a life of joy without the constant political strain that others are burdened with. It allows me to focus on and promote what I love, instead of continually bashing what I hate. This method is far more relaxing on a day-to-day basis, and also relieves a lot of voting day stress. I vote from my home, with an ability to research every single issue with my ballot in hand. Absentee ballots are sent well in advance of voting day, so there is always plenty of time to research, vote and return my ballot so that it may be counted. The rest of the time, I leave politics alone.

There are some issues that are hard to ignore, some news stories that create enough discomfort that I feel that something must be done, immediately. Even if an issue doesn't affect me personally, and there is no way for me to affect change in my local community, I can still write a letter or make a phone call that expresses my opinion to a political body or representative. I take the time to write that letter or make that call, and then I let it go. My family is my first responsibility, which means that I cannot spend time in activism, and I wouldn't want to - as I'm striving to live a life of joy and not dissension. Therefore, I weigh each issue as I come across it, asking myself if it affects me directly, or if I can get involved in a reasonable way in my local community. If not, I write the letter or make the phone call and let it go.

Change your mind

Are you watching history, or are you making it? Seek out trusted sources for news, and resolve to reduce your intake. Let go of the need to be right, instead, ask questions and focus on the process of growth. Be willing to accept someone for who they are without requiring them to feel similarly about religion, politics or any other opinion. If you become aware of a disturbing news report or political issue, write a letter or call a representative, then let it go. Apply to vote absentee so you can better research the issues and vote without added stress.

Day 14: Blissfully Unaware to Empowered Action

"Yep, I feel good about getting that big plumbing job done.", My husband exclaimed. He had just finished a huge job of re-plumbing nearly all the pipe in the basement that ran. from our kitchen and bathroom and had installed a new leech line outside for our home's greywater system. "What do you think?" he asked, a smile on his face. I'm sure he knew, that I knew absolutely nothing about plumbing, but I was pleased as punch that things were draining well. I expressed my thankfulness, but something else had occurred to me. "You know that curvy pipe that goes out from the washing machine so that stagnant air doesn't come back and make the laundry room stinky?" He nodded. Then I said, "Well, is it crazy of me to say that the bathroom gets a little stinky when someone runs water down the kitchen sink?" Danger's eyes got wide. "No, it makes perfect sense!" He then explained to me that the bathroom plumbing was missing one of those "curvy" pipes, also called a P-trap or S-trap. Even with my limited knowledge of plumbing, I had identified an issue with his system and pointed out a way that it could be improved. I was initially concerned that my question would be seen as criticism, but my beau took it in stride, educated

me on proper plumbing terms, and accepted that he would need to correct that part of the job. I was pleased to provide useful feedback, and he was glad to have someone identify a small flaw that could be easily remedied.

> "I think it's very important to have a
> feedback loop. Where you're constantly
> thinking about what you've done, and how
> you could be doing it better.
> I think that's the single best piece of advice:
> constantly be thinking about how you
> could be doing things better and questioning yourself.
>
> You want to be extra rigorous about making
> the best possible thing you can.
> Find everything that's wrong with it And fix it.
> Seek negative feedback,
> particularly from friends."
> - Elon Musk

Who are you? In the most basic of terms, you are human. A bundle of cells and nerve endings and blood streaming in perfect motion to keep your body functioning. You are spirit, and divine at that. A gift of the universe. You may also be a mother, father, child, brother, sister, friend or partner. You may have employment or work for yourself. These are rudimentary labels for our actions and motivations.

While you may have your own idea of what a particular archetype (labels such as daughter, son, mother or father) represents, your actions in that role can differ greatly from your fellow humans. As you age, your identity changes and your motivations and actions within a particular archetype will change. You begin by exploring the world around you, largely dependent upon your parents for your protection, entertainment, and direction. As you age, you begin to test your ability to make your own choices and provide various things for yourself, and as you enter young adulthood you start providing more and more for yourself. Eventually you are completely independent of your parents. While this doesn't usually result in the end of your relationship with them, your reactions to your parents and your needs from them will change significantly.

Ignorance is not bliss, and neither is denial. To grow as a human being, and allow for the utmost clarity in your life, you should analyze each of the roles that you play and how you are affecting the people around you. Asking for feedback is the most direct method of growth in these areas that I am aware of, yet it is also often the most painful.

Asking someone you love how you can improve your relationship with them, may lead to some eye-opening and painful realizations. My eldest daughter once told me that I didn't listen to her enough. It was when she was around 14 years old and struggling with her identity. At the time she listened to music I didn't understand or enjoy, wore clothing I found strange and was at odds with everyone in her family most days. We had a strained relationship at that time, and there were some very rough days wherein I was certain that she'd move out at 18 and I'd never see her again. Something had to change, and while it would have been easier if it had been her, I took on the responsibility of creating a better relationship. As I made an effort to not only listen more, but to also engage in activities with her, and make possible additional situations where we could interact and communicate, tensions eased and we became closer than we had been in years. In asking her for feedback, and acting upon the information she provided, I became a better parent. Through that change, she also became a better communicator. We grew together because I took the initiative by asking her how *I* could improve.

It is far simpler to go through life telling yourself that you're doing the best you can and never ask anyone around you for feedback. During this process you may make some errors in judgment, but you can justify them easily. you can read books on parenting, and implement the nuggets of wisdom you find on those pages. you can get inspired around Valentine's Day to do something sweet or sexy for your partner and you can call mom and dad on important holidays. The problem with this kind of lifestyle is that you stagnate. Reading is empowering, and you can learn through education, but a more direct approach to discovering the areas you can improve upon, is asking others for feedback.

Writers request feedback from their editors prior to publishing their books. They make changes and improve the work before they approach a publisher with their manuscript for review. By the time a publisher sees a manuscript, it has often already been edited several times. If you want your life to be improved, you need to take the *shortest* route to betterment - through acting on feedback.

When people give you feedback, with love and openness, it's important not to react to it immediately. Our natural human tendency is to be defensive. You may deny that you act a certain way, or that your loved one has to walk on egg shells around you, or that you always fight to have the last word. After some time of contemplation, remind yourself that you actually *asked* for this feedback. Realize that even if you do not intend for your behavior to be seen in a certain way, that is how it may be coming across. No matter how good your intentions, if someone around you is getting a certain impression of you, it is *true for them*. You may need to alter your behavior in order to present the best version of yourself possible.

Feedback is a powerful growth tool if you hear it with humility and follow it with action. In asking your children for feedback, you can teach them at a very young age that there is always an opportunity for growth. They then know that their opinions matter, and that there is no fear in creative criticism. I believe that listening to young children is an excellent way to begin this process. They are honest, and their requests aren't usually as painful as those you may receive from adults. A child may ask you to play with them more often, buy more ice cream, or give more hugs (at least, my children did on one occasion). An adult may reveal things about yourself that you aren't quite ready to face, or that are so uncomfortable that you can't imagine them to be true.

Letting go of ego can be difficult because it makes us feel vulnerable. Opening up to change and allowing ourselves the opportunity for growth and learning is empowering. It is a breath of fresh air after years of holding onto self justification for our actions. When you take on the archetype of perpetual student, you allow the universe to bring in opportunities for growth and relationships that will challenge you in remarkable ways.

In chapter 8 we discussed your inner circle, and how important it is to surround yourself with people who will challenge you to greater heights. The process of asking for feedback works well with intentional friendships. Befriending people who are achieving more, earning more and living a more intentional, joyful life, will naturally challenge you to do the same. Asking those same people for feedback will provide you with all the motivation and direction for improvement that you will ever require!

Change your mind

Write a letter or email asking those closest to you, how you can improve. Ask your partner, your children, your business associates, your parents, and your friends. Let them know your intention to grow, and ask them to be as honest as possible without being hurtful. When they reply, listen with your highest self and give their words time to sink in. Take time to reflect on what you hear, without needing to respond to it immediately. On a regular basis, ask your peers how you can improve. Let your desire to learn and improve yourself, be evergreen.

Day 15: Negative SelfTalk to Affirmation

"You are doing such a good job; I'm so proud of you mom!", My 19-year-old daughter encouraged as I trudged up the mountain. Somehow, she had convinced me to run the Warrior Dash with her. Though I wasn't trained to run across the street, much less up a mountain and over obstacles, I agreed. During the run, Kirsten surprised me when she stayed by my side the whole way, going at **my** *pace instead of her much faster, more athletic, (and younger) speed. We climbed wooden contraptions designed to challenge already sore and tired muscles. We swam through mud as thick as oatmeal, then carried that mud for a seeming eternity, up the mountain until rushing down a slide into water so cold it knocked the wind out of our lungs. I crawled on rocky ground, jumped over barriers, wobbled across ropes courses, pulled myself through tunnels, and swam in cold water before I jumped over a fire pit and ran through the finish line! I couldn't have done it without that girl repeatedly telling me that I was doing a fabulous job and how good it would feel when we'd finished. She was amazing! I consider my daughter to be one of the best gifts the universe has ever given me. Sign me up for another race!*

"If you had a friend speak to you
The same way you speak to yourself
How long would you allow that person
To be your "friend"?"
- anonymous

Let me ask you about something deeply personal. How did you talk to *yourself* today? What have you been saying about your actions, your accomplishments or your mistakes? Have you been kind? Have you criticized your choices or errors? Have you called yourself names?

It's time to **stop**!

Let me tell you a story...

Once upon a time, there was a girl. She had a lizard living on her shoulder. Sometimes the lizard would say nice things, but at other times, he would just sit there and poop. That's right; he would poop right on her shoulder. Yuck! No one wants that. No one wants that yucky smelling, disgusting feeling. That's when she would reach up, wash the droppings off, and move on.

You do not need negative self-talk. It does you no good. It's not even motivating! By pointing out behavioral problems in children, speech impediments or stutters, or poor academic performance; those problems get worse instead of better. Children who stutter are particularly susceptible to negative reactions. Their speech will degrade quickly when they are met with discouraging, angry, or frustrated responses from those they're speaking to. In order to help a child overcome their challenges, it's best to treat the child as if those challenges don't exist - or better, to tell them that they are amazing, capable, and awesome! Hint: it works on adults too.

We formulate most of our opinion of ourselves and the world around us by the time we are only 6 years old. A lot of the viewpoints we have about ourselves are instilled in us by our peers, our parents and other adults, even television. If you are exposed to someone who is abusive or emotionally cruel; over time, you may end up believing their words, causing a lasting negative self-viewpoint.

For many years, I was terrified to attend college. It wasn't because I wasn't a good student, or because of the cost, but because I had been told for years that college wasn't for me. I was told "If you go to college, no one will like you.", "College isn't for *you*.", "You don't need to go to school; you're needed at home." So for years, I stayed home and didn't try to go to school.

Then one day I got a job as a waitress, and the owner of the restaurant began affirming me. She would say things like "You are really bright, you should go to college!", "You're such a wonderful person; I'm sure you'd make a lot of friends there." She said these kinds of things to me all the time. She was the most supportive person I'd ever met, and I believe it was her kindnesses, day in and day out that helped to transform me into the woman I am today (P.S. Ellen Wessler - Thank you!). Due to her wonderfully kind words, I drove the 50 miles to the nearest college and signed up for classes.

In a short period of time, I was added to the dean's list, became the president of the Business and Technology Club (I was dual majoring in mathematics & physics), president of the honor society, and founded (and became president of) the drama club. I think I should have started a long time prior, don't you? It was all because of negative comments and subsequent negative self-talk that I didn't go sooner.

The next time your inner voice (i.e. lizard) starts to say something negative, STOP IT. Turn it around by starting with the simple statement, "I am enough". You *are* enough! Today, right now, this minute, you are enough. You can neither change the past nor predict the future. You can create a better world for yourself through your attitude. Be your own biggest fan, beginning today. When things get rough, that is when you need you the most!

One of the most effective methods for changing self-talk is through affirmations. To affirm someone, simply say something nice to them! Encourage them, their dreams, and their positive actions. We affirm our children all the time, even when they're sleeping. I remember my mother telling me when I was little, that when I grew up, I could be whatever I wanted. That was an affirmation!

Self-affirmations are best stated in the positive, using the powerful "I am" and being in the present tense.

I am happier and exude more joy every day.
I am 100% committed to loving life!
I can find joy in every situation.
I enjoy working toward a better ME.

Create affirmations to represent your current self-improvement goals. Read them as part of your morning practice and during your bedtime routine. Paste them up around your home so you see them everywhere you go. Keep a set of note cards in your pocket or purse.

Affirmations may also heal past hurts and negative statements you've been carrying around since childhood. Many of us have had parents, teachers, peers, or other people, say negative things to us as children. We've carried those things around with us throughout our lives. It can be challenging to overcome a weight problem if you were called "fat" as a child, and still think of yourself as a "fat" person. It is possible to overcome a negative self-image with daily affirmations.

Take out two pieces of paper. On one, write negative views about yourself that you've believed for years, and would like to change. On the other, write positive affirmations combating the notions on the first page. Then crumple up the first paper, say "This is *not* me." and throw it away. Read your affirmations daily and witness your spiritual recovery.

> "In a society that profits from your self-doubt,
> Liking yourself is an act of rebellion."
> - Caroline Caldwell

In the 1980's a movement swept across the United States, wherein parents felt they needed to improve the self-esteem of their children. This movement attempted to make children feel happier but removed a lot of their motivation instead. When baseball teams no longer keep score, and everyone "wins", there isn't any motivation for improvement or competition. Instead of handing out participation ribbons, they should have handed out affirmations!

There is a popular stage practice for positivity coaches and self-help gurus, which illustrates the effectiveness of affirmations quite well. A volunteer is brought on stage and asked to close their eyes. The volunteer is then asked to say something like "I am weak and unworthy." ten times. After this, the volunteer is asked to keep their arms up on either side, while the speaker pushes down on their arms. The speaker is easily able to push their arms down every time. Even if the volunteer claims they weren't ready or asks for a second try, the speaker is still able to push their arms down.

Next, the speaker instructs the volunteer to close their eyes once again, and repeat something like "I am a capable and worthy person." ten times. As you can probably guess, the speaker isn't able to push the volunteer's arms down after this exercise!

Words have power! As a child, I was told to say "Sticks and stones may break my bones, but words will never hurt me." whenever a bully said something hurtful or nasty. But it wasn't true. Words do hurt, and the pain lasts well into adulthood.

My children and I recently completed an interesting experiment. I took two clean mason jars and filled them with cooked, white rice. On one jar I wrote the word "LOVE" and allowed the children to decorate the jar. On the other jar, I wrote the word "HATE" and drew an unhappy face. Over the next few days, we would tell the "LOVE" jar that we loved it, "you look so yummy and nutritious!", "Good night rice, I love you!" etc. Conversely, we treated the "HATE" rice unkindly. Whenever someone was upset or frustrated, we told them to put those feelings into the rice in the "HATE" jar.

The two jars of rice sat in the middle of our kitchen table for a few days; then we started seeing the effects of our experiment. The "HATE" rice became moldy, and a gross liquid began collecting at the bottom of the jar. The "LOVE" rice remained white and pure for nearly two weeks while the other rice looked brown, fuzzy and putrid. It shocked our friends and family who came to visit. How powerful our words are! Our children learned a new appreciation for the power of words and learned to speak only kind words as much as possible. Name calling (even in jest) doesn't exist in our home.

Often when we commit to self-improvement, we want to change ourselves overnight. We expect perfection and instant success. While some people can quit smoking one day and never pick up the habit again, for most people, a slow transition is far easier and possibly their only route to success. The Japanese have a principle called "kaizen" in which they practice the art of constant and never ending improvement. The philosophy is that you wake up and are a little bit better today than you were yesterday. Strive to take a few more steps every day, smile a bit more, say one more kind thing, and work a little harder to guard your thoughts against self-deprecation.

Change your mind

Affirm everyone you meet. Say kind things! Keep judgments, negativity and criticism to yourself. Write affirmations that represent your current personal development goals. Include affirmations which offset negative concepts you have been carrying around as false "truths" about yourself. Redefine yourself through affirmations, and read them as often as you are able. Train your brain to *know* that you are a beautiful, powerful part of the divine, and are worthy of love and joy. When your inner self talk turns negative, wipe that sh*t off and move on, with your head held high.

Day 16: Wandering to Aiming the Arrow

"I can't believe you just posted that!", my girlfriend Jennifer typed into the Facebook chatbox. "I'm listening to an old podcast - one that I just never got around to listening to until now. He just said that mastermind groups were integral to success, and if any of the listeners weren't a part of one, they needed to get involved in one as soon as possible." Jennifer is one of my openly entrepreneurial friends. I had just invited her to help me form a new mastermind group, hoping she would be interested. She immediately accepted and sent me the message about the podcast she was listening to at that very moment. So I replied, "What a wonderful synchronicity!" When she messaged me again, she was ecstatic. She said that the podcaster had just said the word synchronicity. And he didn't just say it; he said: "I don't know why, but someone out there needs to hear the word "synchronicity" right now. It was so fun to have our small gathering start on such a high note. Together, she and I had a fantastic series of motivating mastermind calls that lead to all kinds of exciting endeavors, including my writing this book.

"All the world is my school and all humanity is my teacher."
- George Whitman

"If you want to go fast, go alone.
If you want to go far,
Go together."
- African Proverb

Ready, Fire, Aim!

What? That's not your method? It's mine! I often jump into new projects without a plan. Realizing that my interest can be fleeting, I know my best bet for success is to get started quickly. I may make mistakes, but I grow and learn as I do things. It is the best way for *me* to learn just about anything.

I learn by *taking action.*

After years of wanting to write a book, I became rather frustrated with my methods. I would sit down and try to write for hours, most of which was filled with me just sitting and staring at the screen (or out the window). I would end up with a few paragraphs, but not the thousands of words I'd hoped for. I had read that the writing process should be "hard," "pain," or even "hell," and that in order to write you had to sit at a typewriter and "bleed." Writing actually felt like that to me when I tried it, which is why it took me so long to get a book finished.

One day I had an epiphany. If I wanted to learn how to write a book, maybe I should research *how* writers write.

I'm a home educator, and it's a regular occurrence that our family will halt all activity to look up something new. Any time our kids have an interest in something or a question, especially if it's a subject my husband and I know little about, we research it to help our children learn. It's a valuable process because not only do we teach our children *how* to learn, but we learn right along with them. After a day of fun family learning, I realized I could use the same techniques to educate myself on writing technique. Not just from a few angry, negative memes, but from successful writers.

I sat down and started reading about *how* to write a book. I read numerous articles, watched hours of YouTube videos and ordered instructional books. The process didn't match my expectations. I anticipated sitting at my desk for months, squeezing my brain and heart for each word until I had written enough for a "book". Instead, I found proven strategies, organizational techniques, and processes for writing and marketing my work. In the process, I learned that writing a book could be a pleasant and rewarding experience. Each completed chapter prompted celebration in our home!

When you get serious about improving your life, previously inaccessible goals come within your reach. However, to accomplish those goals, you need to learn from the success of others. By learning from masters, you can skip over pitfalls, and skyrocket toward your dreams! You can go from wandering, to aiming your arrow!

It is my hope that after reading this book, you will be empowered to *achieve* your goals. I want to encourage you now to begin the process of learning what it takes to be successful with those goals you've set for yourself. There is a wealth of information out there for you! I guarantee that no matter what you're hoping to achieve for yourself, someone has written a book on the subject, started a podcast or blog about it, or has a course for you to learn what you need to know to be successful.

The whole of human knowledge is at your fingertips. You have no excuse for not pursuing your dreams. If you want to learn to play the violin (one of my personal goals), there are free lessons available online, along with workbooks and music. If you want to learn a foreign language, there are community websites where you can speak with someone in another country to help learn each other's languages. There are YouTube videos, Instructables and many free resources available for any subject you can imagine.

In addition to learning about your goal and the things you want to accomplish, it's a good idea to join a community. Google recently indexed over 620 *million* Facebook groups covering every subject you can imagine. LinkedIn® has many groups with a focus on business interests. You can also use Meetup.com as a wonderful resource for meeting people in your local area who have similar interests and goals. If there isn't a meetup locally, you can easily start one. Communities are forming every day, with people doing exactly what you want to do.

Having accountability partners increases the likelihood that you will achieve a specific goal. By choosing a community of people with similar goals, you'll be far more likely to reach your own. Spending time with joyful people will increase your chances of being happier yourself. The financial investment of taking a class can be an additional motivation while also putting you in touch with like-minded individuals.

Taking action toward your goal is the first step. Begin with baby steps to avoid becoming overwhelmed. Learning from those who have come before you will give you confidence and a straight shot to success. Surround yourself with a community of like-minded individuals providing motivation and support. These are strategies used by successful individuals worldwide to improve themselves and achieve their goals. Goal achievement isn't always easy, but it *is* simple!

The best way to learn a foreign language is via immersion. Immersion is like jumping into the deep end of the pool. It's putting yourself into a situation where everyone around you speaks the language you are trying to learn and *only* that language. Many colleges now offer immersion courses in foreign languages.

Immersion works well for any skill you want to learn, and any goal you want to accomplish. For example, if your goal is to play piano, in addition to taking lessons, you should read books about piano, watch videos, talk to friends about it, and frequent venues where pianists happen to be. Live, eat and breathe your new skill, and you will soon master it!

The more you learn about a particular subject, the less knowledgeable you will feel. However, it's said that if you read for one hour per day in your chosen field, you'll be an expert in 7 years and an international expert in 10 years. It's perfectly acceptable to recognize that you have a lot to learn, but don't let it stop you from making progress.

Change your mind

Let your love for learning and growth be continual. Take a look at your goals and make a plan for self-education. Connect with communities in your area that support your field of study, or your chosen hobby. Read everything you can, watch every video and meet as many experts in your field as you are able. Take the fast lane to achieve your goals while also improving yourself. Meet new people and have *fun*!

Day 17: Failure to Accomplishment

One day while doing dishes, I watched Mel Robbins' TED talk. Later that day, I closed the door to my office and watched it again. Then I started the video and pretended to be watching it for the first time, hoping Danger would notice it, and get sucked in. I shared it on Facebook and watched it again. She wasn't talking to an audience hundreds of miles away. She was talking to me. I had convinced myself that I was "fine". I was "fine" without my goals. I was "fine" sleeping in, not getting any alone time to refill my cup, and being stressed all the time. I was "fine" with dreams that I wasn't working toward, and I was "fine" being out of shape. But I wasn't fine at all. I was struggling. I needed to have someone look me in the eye and tell me that the happiness I was seeking, and the goals I was daydreaming about were on the other side of inertia. I could keep sitting in my chair and not get up, or I could stand and run toward the joy I knew I deserved. I realized that it wasn't around the corner, or on the other side of the fence where the proverbial grass might be greener. No. It was hidden inside me. My poor choices, bad habits and day to day diss-affirmation telling myself that I was "fine" were keeping all the things I wanted in life hidden away, locked behind a four letter word that was a ***complete lie****. I'm not fine any longer. Not now that I'm getting up before the sun, and watching its rays pour over the fields around my house in the morning. Not now that I'm writing a book, marketing it and creating a career. Not now that I'm eating amazing food, and lovingly caring for my body in a new and improved way. No, I'm not fine. I'm fabulous!*

> "If you only ever did the things
> You don't want to do,
> You'd have everything you've ever wanted."
> - Mel Robbins

Now that you've written goals, set a schedule for time spent on achieving those goals, and have surrounded yourself with educational materials and a community, let's help you finish what you've started.

Getting out of bed is hard. The alarm goes off, you groan and hit snooze. It's nice and warm inside your covers, and you see no reason to fix what's not broken. Except, something *is* broken if you're not accomplishing your dreams! Isaac Newton, in all his brilliance, stated that "An object at rest stays at rest." YOU are that object at rest, which is why it's so hard to get out of bed in the morning and start your day. It's also the same reason that it's a challenge to start a new endeavor. Sometimes you're stuck in your comfort zone, and other times you may have "analysis paralysis". Taking action to move forward is just too scary.

Activation energy is the energy required for a chemical reaction in a chemistry experiment. In psychology, it's the energy needed to get you up out of a warm bed and into a cold room. It's also the same amount of energy that it takes you to get started on your goals, work toward a dream or jump into a cold pool. Recently, Tony Robbins was interviewed about his morning routine and explained that he jumps into a freezing pool, shower or body of water first thing in the morning. This chilly action accomplishes several things. The cold water reduces inflammation and wakes up all the nerves in his body, preparing him for movement and exercise. It wakes him up and gives him a thrill first thing in the morning. The best part about his exercise is that it breaks him out of his comfort zone, and gets his mind and body accustomed to initiating the activation energy needed to accomplish his goals.

I'm not suggesting that you take a cold shower every morning (although it's not a bad idea), but I am suggesting you get up in the morning, and jump in the air, splash water on your face or run naked in the snow (try not to get arrested). Do whatever it takes to wake up your cells, and tell your mind and body that today you're going to achieve greatness! To accomplish your goals, you must break your "object at rest" habit and get yourself in motion. Taking that first step will slingshot you into productive action!

In chapter 5 we discussed reverse-engineering your goals. By starting with the end in mind, you can see what you need to accomplish along the way, and make a list of everything required. Then you can create a time line of necessary actions, and a calendar of to-dos. By doing a little bit every day, and by making it a sacred part of your schedule, you will work toward your goals using the

power of Newton's laws. By staying in *motion* toward your goals, you can achieve victory!

During the time you have scheduled for your goal achievement, you absolutely must minimize distractions. Focus completely on your work, your education, practice or exercise. Let those around you know what you're working toward, so that they can support you and give you the time necessary to make your goal a reality.

Track your progress as you work toward your goals. You can make a chart, graph or other visual reminders of your progress. I've seen jars with glass beads that represent pounds to lose, string with mini clothespins to slide over as tasks are completed, and word count apps to measure writing progress. Having a visual representation of your momentum is extremely helpful. If you're unable to come up with a visual representation, or if your goals don't easily facilitate it, you can keep track of how many goal-relevant books you've read, songs you've learned to play, or hours you've spent on a project. A support group can also help to acknowledge any improvement you have made.

Celebrate each level of progress and every small achievement. Jack Canfield recommends keeping a success journal, and writing in it daily. Keeping track of your daily accomplishments can be extraordinarily motivational. It is a real gift to yourself and your goal setting, to be able to see all the good you've done, especially on days when you've lost focus, or have a lack of motivation.

The simple act of checking off items on your To Do list can be equally rewarding. Keeping a small notebook or journal, and taking the time every evening to write down what I DID accomplish, instead of focusing on any remaining tasks, is one of the best things I've ever done to combat feeling overwhelmed. I am able to look at that list, however small, and know that I took steps toward my goals, performed some feats of domestic goddessness, kissed boo boos and snuggled the hubby. This list is my gift to that inner mom who feels guilty for not doing enough. She needs gentle reminders that she already IS enough.

Perfectionism can slow you down, and cripple your ability to achieve your goals. As a perfectionist, I've given up on things in the past, simply because I could tell that my way of doing it wasn't perfect. I waited months to finish painting my living room because one small piece of wood trim was missing. I even put off a family vacation, because I allowed little things I deemed "imperfect" to keep me from enjoying the opportunity. I cannot live this way any longer, and neither can you. It steals your joy! You may think that the only way of doing something is to do it perfectly, but it's not the only way. Thinking in this manner will stop you from achieving your goals.

Remember that life isn't about the destination; it's the journey that matters. Every small step is progress. Also, keep in mind that a mediocre product, developed and launched, is better than no product at all. A small amount of exercise is better than sitting on your tail all day. Eating a cookie with your salad is better than avoiding salad altogether. I have to remind myself of these small things every day. By completing my torch running task, taking another step toward my goals, and letting go of perfection, I can accomplish great things, and you can too.

Lastly, know your "why". Take a moment to write down *why* you want to accomplish the goal you're working on. Is it to improve yourself or your health? To increase wealth or achieve admiration? Is it simply to check an experience off your bucket list? The more compelling your reason for reaching a goal, and the more frequently you remind yourself of that reason, the faster and easier it will be for you to achieve it. It takes only a moment to write down your why. Spend a few minutes in your morning and evening practices reminding yourself of your reason. This small amount of time creates the *emotional attachment* to your goal, which is necessary for achievement.

Change your mind

Ask yourself why you want to accomplish your goals, and write down your answers. Every morning, get yourself pumped up, and in the *motion* of achievement. It starts with completing your daily torch running task, and recording that success for the day. Celebrate your successes no matter how small - ("Yay, I did a load of laundry and we don't have to be naked this week!"). Keep track of your daily progress toward your goals, so you have a visual motivation tool. Do your best to let go of perfectionism, and ditch inaction for achievement!

Day 18: Worry to Courage

"I'm worried that Voldemort will come." "Oh, sweety! Voldemort isn't real; he was invented by the author of the book. She just made him up in her head, and he doesn't exist." I said to my frightened 5-year-old daughter. "But I'm still scared that he will come and hurt my sisters." "I can promise that he won't come." I replied. "Promise?" "Promise." I hugged her and gave her a flashlight, and she snuggled into bed. I could tell that she was still worried, still doubting that Voldemort didn't exist at all, even if he was just a character in a book. It's been months since that first night of concern, and my daughter is still quite worried every night that the antagonist of the Harry Potter series is going to come into our home in the middle of the night and do some magical harm to our family. Every night she wakes and runs, crying through the house, to our bed and snuggles between my husband and me before falling back to sleep. Oh, how I wish I could pluck that fear and worry from her, so she could experience even one night of blissful rest. But it's her fear, and I can't. No matter how many conversations we have about this character, she is still dubious that he

doesn't exist.

> "Worry does not empty tomorrow of its sorrow.
> It empties today of its strength."
> - Corrie ten Boom

> "If a problem is fixable, if a situation is such that you can do something
> About it, then there is no need to worry. If it's not fixable, then there's no
> Help in worrying. There is no benefit in worrying whatsoever."
> - His Holiness the Dalai Lama XIV

I once heard a story of an elderly man nearing his death. When asked what he most regretted, he admitted that it was all the wasted time worrying. He said that most of what he feared, had never happened, so all that energy wasted in worry could have been used for so much more. It's easy for us to get carried away with worry. Our mind tends to imagine the worst, when the unknown is on the horizon.

I remember hearing that my ex-husband was going to sue me for custody of our children. The blow was unexpected, and devastating emotionally. Fear and worry gripped me for weeks. Statistics showing that most women win custody battles didn't help, my supportive husband didn't help, even my positive attorney couldn't stem the worry and fear that I had. The thought of losing my children was so terrifying that it clouded my reason and sapped my joy for weeks.

The case did not end the way I'd imagined, of course. Instead, he dropped the case halfway through. I was surprised to hear that they found my evidence compelling, and thus ended the suit. It was the most painful thing I've ever endured, but all of the pain came from a worry that never happened. My mind conjured the worst-case-scenario and held onto it like a nightmare I couldn't wake from.

Most of the things you will worry about will never happen at all. How sad is it that we allow these phantom ideas to take over so much of our energy, and cause us both mental and physical harm? Yes, the stress from worry is physically harmful. Stress is hard on your heart and other body systems. It weakens you and hampers your needed rest. It puts your body on high alert as if you were fighting a virus. Long term, it can cause severe harm or even death.

Reducing worry starts with knowing that the worst case scenario isn't the most likely outcome. That being said, if you know what the worst case scenario is, and you see that it's survivable, it can help to reduce the stress from worry. Tell yourself that the outcome your brain is coming up with isn't likely, and that even if it is, it's probably survivable. Be encouraged that others have been there before you, which can help to mitigate anxiety.

Start by defining what exactly you are worrying about. Write it down and look at it. By precisely identifying your concerns, you reduce vague fears to something tangible. Make your concerns as detailed as possible so that they can be addressed. Worrying about the unknown is a constant battle with no end. Once it's tangible, you can ask for assistance or advice. It's a stepping stone toward eliminating that fear or worry.

1. Define your worry.
2. Make your concerns as specific as possible.
3. Ask for assistance or advice.

When your worries involve other people, especially their thoughts and motivations, you have to take care to not assume what they are thinking. Your judgment of their actions can easily be misplaced or misunderstood - especially when taken out of context or when judging comments made online or via text. You need to caution yourself not to jump to conclusions, but instead to ask for clarification. Speak directly to that person, letting them know that you're concerned about something. Give them a chance to help, rectify the situation or elaborate on their actions or words.

Seeking clarity in your relationships, especially after an awkward interaction, is the only way to heal a hurt or wrongdoing. By holding onto grudges, concerns and frustrations, you are holding a grenade of stress that will harm you most of all. Clarification will probably reveal that your judgment was unfounded or mistaken. It's far better to be wrong about someone's intentions when you feel hurt than to learn that their actions were intentionally harmful, which is quite rare. People are generally kind and good, but miscommunication and misunderstanding leads to unnecessary conflict.

When your mind starts racing with worry, and your fears come to the surface in the worst way, sometimes you just have to shout STOP!! There are times when you need to take control of your own mind. Mothers often worry about their children, and I'm no exception. There have been nights when I'm trying to drift off to sleep, and my mind begins racing with horrible things that could happen to my sweet children. It often gets worse and worse until I have to take a deep breath and STOP that junk.

Mindfulness comes in handy in these situations. It's at this time that you look around you and ask yourself "What is *really* happening right now?". Are you safe, warm, happy, and healthy? That is what matters most right now. These fears and worries are just figments of your imagination!

Most of the time when you are concerned about people in a crowd, worried about your appearance, or how you're coming across in an interview, you need to recognize that for the most part, people are all thinking about themselves. Recently I attended my husband's 25th high school class reunion. After the first night, he asked me if anyone would notice if he washed and re-wore his favorite dress shirt. I thought for a few moments about the other men at the gathering, and we both realized that we couldn't remember what most of them were wearing, especially those whose clothing wasn't particularly striking or labeled. He wore the shirt the next night, and no one noticed (at least, they didn't mention it if they did).

This particular concept would help young people the most. Statistically, you care less about what others think as you age. Nevertheless, it's still a concern, especially for women. Reminding yourself that most other people are thinking about themselves, and are generally unconcerned about your appearance or actions, is quite the comfort.

Exercise is one of the most effective cures for worry and stress that exists. For many people, making time for exercise is a challenge. However, if worry and stress are on your plate, you need to make the time. I personally like to get mine done in the morning, before anyone else wakes up, but I also find afternoon to be a nice time to exercise. If you have children, you can exercise or take a walk *with* them. Not only will you be providing an excellent example, but also opportunities for their own loving movement.

There are times when the aforementioned techniques (employing rational thinking, defining our worries, and exercising) don't relieve all the worry and stress from our lives. In this case, it helps to talk to someone about our worries. My first choice is my extremely supportive husband. He's always available for me to talk to, and he happens to be my number one fan. At any time I'm concerned or worried, he's also the first person to talk me off of the worry ledge, and bring me down to a more mindful approach to whatever is bothering me. In addition to my sweet husband, my best friends Kayla and Ruth listen and commiserate, which is also a wonderful gift. Just having someone listen and give a hug (even if it's virtual) can make a world of difference to someone who's struggling.

There is nothing wrong with seeking a professional to talk to. When I was going through my divorce, I spoke to a counselor weekly. He helped me work through my feelings and pain, and gave me tools to build strength and self confidence. Many of us have grown up without tools for relieving stress, depression, and anxiety. A mental health professional can educate you so that you can help yourself. When things are more than we can handle, and those tools aren't working, those same professionals can suggest medication for those who need it. Lives are saved by mental health professionals. Even if you don't feel you need that kind of support, know that they are available and discreet.

In the end, life continues. The Earth still moves and the sun still rises. Which means that you must keep moving yourself. On those days when you feel overwhelmed, when worry or stress take over, just do one thing at a time. Pick one thing up and put it away. Give one hug, make one phone call, or smile once in the mirror. Just do the next right thing, and then the next, until you get through. Remember that emotions are only temporary after all, and this too shall pass.

Change your mind

Worry is living in the future. It's often wasted energy that could be better spent living our lives with joy. When you are faced with a worry (which can hit at any time, and be big or small), define it and write it down in your journal. Seek clarity, support, and assistance when and if you need to. Keep in mind that emotion is temporary, and most of us spend the majority of our lives in a state of contentment that is neither an extreme joy nor a despair. If worry is overwhelming you, and following the above suggestions isn't helping, seek professional help so you can heal.

Day 19: Regret to Acceptance

A familiar stage act for self-help speakers who are trying to convey the pain of regret, is to ask for a volunteer. There are many people in the audience who immediately raise their hands, and many more that want to raise their hands, but don't. The speaker asks the audience again for a volunteer, and more hands shoot up. They still don't get it, so the speaker asks for a volunteer a third time. At this, one or two people finally get up and run toward the stage. The person that gets there first is rewarded with a crisp new bill (the amounts differ, I've seen $20, $100 or £50). The speaker then advises the volunteer to return to their seat and proceeds to chastise the crowd for not acting on their interest in volunteering. They also point out that those people who wanted to come up to the stage but didn't, are now feeling regret because they missed out on the money.

"The past is a great place and I
don't want to erase it, or to regret it,
but I don't want to be it's

prisoner either."
- Mick Jagger

"Do not brood over your past mistakes and failures
as this will only fill your mind with grief,
regret, and depression.
Do not repeat them in the future."
- Swami Sivananda

Worry and regret go hand in hand. When you worry, you're thinking about the future. When you are filled with regret, you're thinking of the past. Bringing yourself to a state of mindful awareness of the present is essential for lasting joy.

Regret is particularly insidious because we enjoy it. Not only do we personally appreciate regret, but we encourage it in the people around us, even in our children. We find value in regret. As a culture, we consider regret a symbol of the lesson learned from wrongdoing. Oddly, we value regret even more than pride. Regret is seen as valuable and justifiable. As individuals, it keeps us in check with morality.

The problem with regret being an honorable emotion is that it's quite painful. Wallowing in it can be detrimental to our peace and joy, over time. While regret has its purpose and place, and it can be seen as a beneficial tool, to learn from our mistakes, the pain it generates over time can cause lasting damage to us psychologically. You have to move on eventually and let go.

A recent study showed that women are more likely to regret

emotional mistakes. Mistakes in relationships, sex, and parenting are our most challenging. Men, however, tend to dwell on mistakes of a more financial nature. They will remember more harshly their errors in judgment when it comes to education or their career than other mistakes they may have made. But, the #1 regret for all people is **missed opportunity**.

Lamenting things you didn't do or missed out on, is more painful than remembering mistakes you've made. Your mind has natural defenses built in. When something bad happens to you, or around you, your mind immediately gets to work helping you cope with the situation. In the event of a poor choice, your mind immediately looks for silver linings to your errors in judgment. If you made a mistake while driving that resulted in a car accident, your mind would focus on the fact that you lived through the event. You'd be filled with feelings of regret for your mistake, but also feelings of relief that it wasn't as bad as it could have been. In the event of a painful divorce, your mind may focus on the beautiful children you still have to share your life with, instead of the years of a painful relationship that ended in failure.

Why is it so hard for us to rationalize missed opportunity? It's because it's hard to learn from an experience if there is *no experience* to learn from. Imagine if your senior prom date had spontaneously asked you to marry them, but you declined. Then, that same person grows to become wealthy and famous. It is painful to imagine what "could have been," because you have no idea how good or bad, that relationship might have been. Imagine being the prom date for Angelina Jolie or Brad Pitt, and how challenging watching them become famous and successful would have been.

Surprisingly, regret is simple to self-correct. When you find yourself wallowing in misery over a mistake you've made (we've all been there), remember to ask yourself the following two questions:

1. What can I learn from this experience?

and

2. How could it have been worse?

By asking yourself what you could learn from the experience, you're giving regret a purpose. Regret is a useful tool to help us to learn from our mistakes. The lesson should always be addressed. By focusing on the lesson of the experience, you're able to move forward as a better person than you were the day before, which is all anyone can hope for. This is how learning from your mistakes takes place. You can do this on your own, or with help from others.

A while ago, I spent a couple of weeks engrossed in a video game. The game consumed a lot of my waking hours, whenever I could squeeze in time to play it. I turned my computer on first thing in the morning and played the game, I played after lunch and again in the evening. It was all consuming! I was thinking about the game all the time, whether I was playing or not. One day, scrolling through Pinterest on my phone while waiting in line at the grocery store, I saw an infographic of the back of a woman's head as she sat at the computer. Below was the question "Do you want your children's earliest memories to be of the back of your head? Game responsibly." That hit me like a ton of bricks.

I stopped playing the game immediately, and uninstalled it from my computer. I felt shame and regret for having spent so much time engrossed in something that wasn't even real, and possibly neglecting my family as I did so. However, I learned from my experience, and my regret. I learned that my family is more important to me than any game. I learned that there are a lot of other things I'd rather be doing than sitting at my computer. I was also reminded of how detrimental computer games can be to relationships and our physique. There are ways to manage your time so that if you are a person who enjoys games you can still play them and also have plenty of time for your family. Personally, I have a hard time limiting my gaming time, so I need accountability or hard rules like "No indulging when my children are awake". *They* are my priority.

After asking what you can learn from your experience, ask yourself "How could it have been worse?" This question is essential for particularly unfortunate situations. It helps our brain find the silver lining. There are small bits of good in every situation, you just need to actively look for them.

Lastly, you must do your best to avoid regret by making wise choices. Cultivate a mental attitude of wisdom, and make the best decisions you can, on a daily basis. Tell yourself that you are wise. Praise your children for their good choices and kind actions. Give them a reason to believe that they are good people who make wise choices. Listen to your intuition and go with your gut instinct. Be moderate in your consumption of anything that may reduce your ability to make wise choices.

The most important change you can make right now to reduce

regret for missed opportunity is to **act**. Like Nike says "Just Do It". If it won't result in death, bodily harm, divorce or incarceration, DO IT. Take the chance that you're contemplating. *Do the thing.* In the end, you'll have more regret for *not* taking action than you'll have for any failure. Failing isn't as painful as missing the opportunity altogether.

You are worth it!
You can do it!
You deserve it!
And you **will** be better off, for taking the leap!

A few years ago, Danger and I attended Burning Man. If you're unfamiliar with the event, it's an 8-day camping art festival in the Nevada desert. During the day, there are sand storms and extreme heat. The desert is full of massive art projects from all over the world. At night, the desert is lit up, and music is everywhere. It was an amazing experience all around. One of the things that impacted me was the spirit of radical inclusion. Everyone is invited to everything. There are people cooking pancakes for anyone who happens by their camp, giant swings and rides that you can play on, and art cars waiting to be clambered upon and ridden. We rode in a car that was shaped like a bowl of cereal, complete with Fruit Loop pillows. We did silly things and crazy things, and we were included in everything we saw. Our initial tendency was to be timid and observational, but after about 24 hours we were jumping in and playing like everyone else. Every night ended with smiles, and every morning began as a spiritual gift. We made friends and memories, and I'm incredibly thankful for the experience. I'm glad I didn't miss that opportunity!

Change your mind

If you are struggling with regret right now, ask yourself how you can learn from the situation. Give yourself the opportunity to be better tomorrow than you were today, and honor the improved you. Ask how it could have been worse, and find the silver lining. Allow yourself the gift of knowing that it wasn't as bad as it could have been so that you may heal and move forward.

Jump on the bus toward opportunity! Allow yourself the risk of failure, because the loss of opportunity will feel worse than the failure ever could. Get **out** of your comfort zone on a regular basis. Listen to your instincts, and allow your higher self to guide you to new opportunities.

Day 20: A Divine Mindset

It's easy to see people as different from you. They might be in a wheelchair, have crutches, or have different skin or hair. They may have an injury that you're curious about, or they might be sad, and you may wonder why. When you meet others that are different, the good news is that the differences you perceive are only outward. On the inside, we're all the same: A beautiful, bright, loving spirit. Our bodies are gloriously unique, but the truth is that we are far more alike than we are different! We can always use that fact to bond us to people we're just meeting, to build curiosity and trust, and most of all, to cultivate empathy.

"I am in you, and you are in me,
Mutual in divine love."
- William Blake

"The cosmos is within us.
We are made of star-stuff.
We are a way for the universe to know itself."
- Carl Sagan

You are star dust! Every element that makes up the universe (and everything in it), is also present inside of you. This means that you are related to the trees, the animals, and everything else on this planet and beyond. If every moment you were reminded of your divine nature, and that of the people around you, how would it change your actions and thoughts? How much different could the world be if we saw each other in this light?

You are divine love manifested into physical form! Love created you and inspires you. Look at your situation, your body, your future and past, all *through the lens* of love. If you view your existence through this lens, you can be kinder to yourself. You will realize that you are enough, just as you are. Any errors in judgment, any mistakes you think you are making, any poor choices - they matter far less than you think. Most of our negative self-talk is directed at ourselves after a rather insignificant mistake.

I often tell my guests that "We know the supper is ready when the smoke alarm goes off!" Years ago, when I was struggling to love myself, I would become furious if I became distracted and overcooked any food. Burnt bacon may have been the worst thing in my mind. I would berate myself repeatedly for that kind of mistake. At the time, I should have pointed out that burnt bacon doesn't matter in the grand scheme of things, and no one is likely to remember it! I was harsh with myself for the smallest of mistakes.

I'm looking at myself (and my mistakes) through a better lens now. I can see that these small mistakes no longer matter in the long run. It's far better to laugh and move on, than it is to get so worked up over these small errors.

Looking at someone else's life through your lens of divine love gives you the patient perspective of empathy and kindness. It allows you to see their actions as their own - without you feeling personally responsible. It also gives you the freedom of letting other beings be themselves, without needing them to fit inside your perceived requirements for behavior or character. You will instead see them as divine beings themselves, on their own path of exploration through life.

Love is wonderfully universal. Love is the most important tenant of nearly every religion, and it transcends language and culture easily. When you walk the Earth with your divine light as your guide, it will not matter where you happen to be, the rest of the people around you will see and feel it. They will be moved by your presence.

Imagine the light from your being filling the space you're sitting in right now. Imagine it filling the room you are in, and then the building. Imagine that it sweeps out over your neighborhood and city. Then, envision it enveloping the entire Earth. Your love is bigger than even that. Love does not stop at the edges of your body, nor your front door. It reaches to all the people in your life and beyond. You can send your love (energy, thoughts, prayers) to anyone or anything you wish.

Prayer, energy work, etc. works to speed up healing, to uplift moods and to ease tensions between people. Whatever word you have for sending your love to others, use it daily. Be generous with your love, and give it freely to everyone you meet.

While focusing on your divine light and love, you can practice empathy in new ways. You can think of people, philosophies, religious views and political views from a position of love. You can see someone's opposing point of view, without being concerned that it could threaten you in any way. By meditating upon this, you can release yourself from negative feelings toward those people or groups.

A short meditation: Take a moment to think of someone who is causing you frustration. Allow yourself to focus on your Divine light and love when you're concentrating on this person. See them through that lens, and imagine your love surrounding them as well. Then put yourself in their place, and imagine how they may feel, or what may have brought them to their particular viewpoint. Allow yourself to feel not just their perspective, but your love flowing into that different viewpoint. Then come back to yourself, but continue to love that person where they are. Release the vision and take a deep breath.

Being of universal divine origin, you are co-creator of your life and the world around you. Once you have taken responsibility for your choices (see day 1) and have written goals that you've reverse-engineered, you can use your divine nature to change your life for the better. All you need is a bit of affirmation, visualization and *emotion* to bring about lasting change in your life. The key to making things happen, to creating with prayer or goals, is to *feel* the emotion you would feel when your life has changed according to that goal, dream, prayer or wish.

Many people have trouble with visualization. When trying to imagine their life without financial struggle, living in their dream home and enjoying a happy life, they claim to have trouble coming up with the images in their mind. I bet I can describe a situation wherein you won't have any trouble picturing in your mind's eye what I'm thinking:

Imagine a man yawning and scratching, walking through a dark house in his pajamas. When he reaches the kitchen, he yelps in pain as he steps on a lego® left by his toddler earlier that evening. When he turns on the light, he is surprised to find the whole floor covered in legos®! Instead of tip-toeing across the little plastic land mine-laden floor, he pirouettes on the spot and dances gracefully on his toes to the refrigerator. He then reaches into the freezer for the ice cream, turns around and prances his way to get a spoon with a huge grin on his face.

Could you picture that silly scene? All you need is the proper picture. Don't think of pink elephants! See, again, I've now placed an image into your mind. Visualization is as simple as recalling the dream you had last night, picturing a fiction book scene in your head, or thinking about a great Olympics event. It's just placing pictures in your mind, preferably that stimulate as many of your senses as possible. When we visualize for our dreams and goals, this is exactly what we're doing. Let's try a more relevant example:

You pull up to the White House in your meticulous new, black Bugatti Veyron. A sharp-dressed valet opens your door and requests your invitation, which you promptly produce. You are invited to exit your vehicle and you step out onto the gravel drive at 1600 Pennsylvania Avenue, NW. It is a perfect evening, with a beautiful clear sky. You can smell sweet flowers from the presidential gardens and delicious scents coming from the White House kitchens. As you walk toward the pillared entrance, your dress sweeps gently against the ground. You feel stunning and confident in your Alexander Wang Balenciaga gown, and heads turn at your arrival. After the security checkpoint, you enter the White House and are greeted by a host of celebrities, offered delicious gourmet hors d'oeuvres and champagne.

At long last the President himself enters the room, and immediately heads toward you. He takes your hand and brings it to his lips for a polite kiss, and tells you that he is so very glad that you could make it. You are the honored guest, the largest contributor to a charity you feel very strongly about. Your heart surges with pride and pleasure as you realize that your contribution will help so many people. At supper, you chit-chat with the President and First Lady about your career and success. After dancing and enjoying the company of celebrities and other contributors you head home, elated.

Imagining any goal, in a detailed and pleasurable way, can give you the much-needed drive to complete all the small tasks necessary to achieve it. Visualizing a frightening situation in a funny way (like a speaker imagining his audience naked) can give you confidence and security. Similarly, athletes will imagine perfect pole vaults and how they will feel when the gold metal is placed around their neck. Visualization is so powerful that it affects the same centers in the brain, and even stimulates the same muscles that will be used in the actual event!

When you want to manifest something into your life, it's best to describe it as fully as you are able. Use images from the Internet, drawings, or lists that you've created that describe your vision. Then imagine what it will *feel* like when that vision becomes reality. That feeling of excitement, joy, elation - that is what is needed to make the Law of Attraction work. The Law of Attraction is you using your divine creative gift to change the world around you!

Change your mind

You are divine light. Fill your room, your home, your community, city and country with your loving light. It is not bound by the flesh of your body, but is limitless! Use this love and light as a lens to view the world with. Share your love! Accept that you have the gift of divine creation within you, and use it to create the life you want through visualization and joyful emotion. Step into your greatness!

Mindset
practices

Ten simple mindfulness practices to bring your mind to the present and *unleash* your *joy*.

"The present moment is filled with joy and happiness.
If you are attentive, you will see it."
- Thích Nhất Hạnh

"In this moment, there is plenty of time.
In this moment, you are precisely as you should be.
In this moment, there is infinite possibility."
- Victoria Moran, Younger By The Day

DAY 21: THE MINUTIAE

My husband once said, early in our relationship, that it was the changes the house took on that were the most significant. He would come home from work and find a toy in the yard, decorative pumpkins on the porch or lights strung up, and he would know that they weren't there when he had left for work. It was in those moments that he was thankful to have our "instant" family (I came pre-packaged with two cool kids). Now that we have three more children together, the house isn't the same from hour to hour, much less, day to day. At night, when the house is quiet, you can walk around and see the dramatic change that every room has taken on, in the wake of family life. As I walk through and re-fold blankets, pick up toys, and straighten things, I smile to see all the loving chaos that is left behind by children. I also find my home, in the quiet of the night, buzzing in an almost audible whisper, of the energy and giggles that were so pervasive just hours before. To acknowledge that this home holds more than just material things, but also memories, joys, tears, and the heart of our familial love, is a ***gift*** *to us as well as the timbers and nails that hold it together. What an honor it is, to live in a 100-year-old farmhouse that has historically housed big, happy families! Interestingly, the two most recent families preceding ours* *had three daughters each as well. There are still secrets to be found here, and I intend to learn them all.*

"The true secret of happiness
Lies in taking a genuine interest
In all the details of daily life."
- William Morris

Tiny objects fascinate my daughter, Amelie. Ever since she was a baby, her preference has been the tiniest toys, smallest utensils, and tiny leaves, and rocks that she can find in the yard. When gardening, she enjoys planting the smallest seeds and will focus intently on each minuscule lettuce and onion seed as it's placed perfectly by her small fingers. She has grown to be extremely detail oriented, as you can imagine, but being focused on the smallest things around her has given her another benefit - peace.

Amelie is my most joyful child. It takes a lot more to bother her or shake her spirit than anyone I know. She also leaves little reminders of her presence all over our home. When I enter the kitchen expecting to cut a fresh-baked loaf of bread for lunch, I find a pebble-sized toy on my cutting board. When I open a window for fresh air, I find a small plastic bear or bird on the sill, oriented as if it's looking outside. When I enter the bathroom to brush my teeth at night, there's a tiny metal disk on the vanity, some forgotten piece of farm equipment dug up by Amelie on our property. Her little deposits bring us all an immense amount of joy.

When you focus on miniature, detailed things, your mind slows down. You'll step out of the rush of life and into another world. For a brief period of time, the ruts in tree bark can become vast chasms for us to explore. You can recognize how the internal structure of a leaf, when viewed in the sunshine, is very similar to the veins under your own skin.

People go through life being rather oblivious to so much around them. You may sit at a desk for years without ever appreciating the woodgrain in its surface. You might work in a room without noticing chips in the paint or the way the sun's rays move across the space throughout the day. You could live in a home for 20 years and never spend 5 minutes admiring the bark of a tree in the front yard.

Our modern world is busy and confusing. Before I go to bed, I create a to-do list for the following day. I spend a good deal of time thinking about tomorrow's plans. When morning arrives, my natural inclination is to be hurried, anxious for coffee, and hoping for some quiet and solitude before the daily rush begins. Focusing on a small detail, allows me to slow down and pay attention to the world around me before I jump in and start my torch running task.

I've lived in this house now for over ten years. I still notice new things that were oblivious to me for years. Since its 1918 construction, it's been added on to, renovated, and decorated many times. The property and the flora and fauna on it have changed over the years significantly. The barn has begun to sag and droop from the weight of so many years of use. Just this week I noticed a patched portion of the wall of our back bedroom and realized that a previous owner had altered that part of the wall. I moved our bed to discover that the window behind it was quite a bit larger in the past, as evidenced by the subtle outline in the restored wall around it.

A contractor would have likely noticed these things much sooner than I. But I also noticed new cherry tree sprouts near where the old cherry tree (now several years dead and gone) once stood. I noticed that there were wasps flitting around a tree that was dead and scheduled for removal, and upon closer inspection we discovered more than two hives living in the tree stump. We've learned that the lilac bushes on the back corner don't get enough water or sunlight, that the ideal position for our garden is near the front drive, and that the dining room gets too warm in the autumn.

These are small things about our home that we've noticed quite recently, after engaging in a desire to more deeply understand our home and property. Noticing very small things around you, touching them, and interacting with them, will give you a greater appreciation for those things. When de-cluttering, holding an object and focusing on it to see if it brings you joy is an excellent way to determine whether or not it belongs in your home. Holding and appreciating something that was a gift, or belonged to a loved one who has passed on, can bring comfort and hope.

One of my favorite things to do with my newborns was just to sit and examine their little fingers and toes, their facial features, ears, and tummies. I tried to memorize every wrinkle and roll. To relish every breath they took and every dreamy sigh. The tiny hairs on their head and the itty bitty nails on their digits inspired delight.

Now I do the same thing from time to time with my husband. I seek out opportunities to glimpse small changes aging has imposed.

I see the gray hairs he's gained since our marriage and the tiny lines that form at the corners of his eyes when he smiles. Noticing and appreciating these small details fills me with joy and appreciation. They are reminders of a shared and beautiful history. These visible symbols represent our life together, our adventures, and our struggles. They are precious to me.

When I was in my deepest, darkest moments of depression, I found solace in the oddest things. Since my mind betrayed me at every opportunity with dark, sad thoughts, I needed a way to distract her. I found comfort during these times by focusing on the minutiae around me. The twisting knots of a crocheted sweater, the threads on my comforter, the grain of a wood table next to me. I became fixated on wallpaper patterns, some of which were entrancing, and others stomach-turning.

I encourage you to mindfully explore the world around you, with the goal of seeing the details. Watch your child's face as they concentrate on a project. Look at the steam as it wisps upward from your mug of coffee in the morning. Notice pink cheeks and noses in the winter, and sun-kissed shoulders in the summer. Appreciate your belongings in a new way, by studying the details. Run your hands along the walls of your home. While expressing gratitude for your residence, pay attention to the tiny joys your home offers.

The next time a child takes a crayon to the wall, leave their artwork for a day or two. Sit down at their level and touch the marks. Wonder at what they were thinking when they created this "art".

If you focus on one small thing per day, and wholly devote yourself to its examination for a few minutes, it is an act of meditation. It slows you down and allows you to escape from the hustle of modern life. It is the silence of the "in between" that you're seeking:

> That time after a thought passes before another has begun.
> The quiet that is present in the grooves of skin on your knuckle.
> The place where a pine needle attaches to the branch.
> The way a rock feels in your hand when you close your eyes and run your fingers along its surface.

Your mindfulness practice

Notice the details around you. Take a bit of time every day to touch, observe and explore your environment. Be mindful in this time. Be wholly present in the current moment, without care for the past or the future. Just **be**. Like the object you're observing, you are simply part of your environment, nothing more, nothing less. Allow that simplicity to bring peace and rest. There are no requirements in it.

You are enough.

Day 22: Green Growth

I have two rules for outside play. Don't climb a tree you can't climb down yourself, and if you get your feet stuck in the mud, you're required to pull the muddy socks and shoes out and bring them back inside so they can be washed with the rest of you. Now, go play!

"Look deep into nature,
And then you will understand everything better."
- Albert Einstein

"Earth and sky, woods and fields,
Lakes and rivers, the mountain and the sea,
Are excellent schoolmasters,
And teach some of us more than we can ever learn from books."
- John Lubbock

When I was a child, I recall making a fort under an evergreen tree, weaving bracelets and crowns from grass and flower stems. I ran and adventured in the forest behind my grandmother's country home, and ate blackberries growing in her front yard. I picked peas from my father's garden and stuffed them into my mouth when he wasn't looking. Habitually barefoot, I once stepped on a bee and got stung between my toes. I spent nearly every waking moment outside. There were hours of bike riding, and investigating the local creek bed. Role playing with neighbor kids, and street hockey were a regularity. I had no fear of bugs or discomfort from dirt. My heart and mind were wholly occupied with adventure, princes on their white horses, and the glorious beauty in nature. I rolled down grassy hills, climbed trees, and jumped into lakes.

As I aged, I somehow became more uncomfortable with nature. I withdrew from it and even developed an aversion to it. I stopped rolling down hills, having picnics, and weaving crowns. I worried about bugs and dirt and ticks and gross, icky, yucky things. I focused on technology, clean hands and faces, and always wearing shoes. I grew up… or thought I had.

I even imposed these new restrictions on my children. They always had to have shoes on, faces and hands washed. I kept baby wipes in my car and purse, so I could eliminate the tiniest bit of dirt that contaminated their skin. I didn't let them play outside if it was muddy or too cold. The saddest part about it was that I *knew* it was unfair and unhealthy to make those decisions. I regretted every one of them. I missed going out and getting messy! My children needed more time outside for their healthy development. When I did allow them out to play, all of us were happier, and I learned for myself, that going outside was worth the risk. I nearly always had fun, found something beautiful or interesting, or was simply uplifted and refreshed afterward.

I remember meeting other families with "free range" children. Kids who never wore shoes or who always had messy faces and unkempt hair. It was uncomfortable to see parents who had so little *control* of their children until I realized that there was **joy** there. That these parents were picking battles far more important than dirty toes and tangles. These children were wild and free, but they were also learning and experiencing life in a rewarding and exciting way. My children were proper and well-mannered, which I was proud of, but I began seeking a compromise between my need for control, and the importance of freedom and a healthy dose of nature.

In my journey toward physical and mental wellness, I've learned that nature plays a large role in the morale of human beings. Corporations add plants to their offices because people **need** a little nature in their lives to be sane and productive. Large companies like Google are creating small parks for their employees to enjoy during breaks and encouraging them to bring their laptops into the sunshine to work outside. Taking just 15 minutes to stroll in an area with trees will boost your ability to focus and be more creative.

Mindfulness practices that involve nature are extremely effective. People are naturally drawn toward and uplifted by living plants. Getting outside and focusing on the plants and trees, the sunshine and clouds, and singing birds, provides you with a rejuvenating focus.

I adore the relaxing sound of water, and I treasure rainy days. The smell and sound of rain immediately calm me, and I find myself inspired to play, write and create. I recently purchased a desktop fountain, and it creates a wonderful atmosphere in my office. I've used a nature sounds app on my phone to reduce stress while waiting at Doctor's offices or the DMV, and my children often fall asleep faster, and sleep better, when listening to whale calls or other nature recordings.

A huge portion of today's adults suffer from insomnia. It's widely known that spending time in nature, without technology, for as little as a few days can heal our circadian rhythm and put us on a healthier sleeping schedule. However, it's rare that we take time to de-tech and return to the Earth's natural light and dark cycle. No matter how many studies point out that indulging in any back-lit screened entertainment after dark will harm your ability to rest, we continue to watch late night television, surf the internet and browse social media on our phones.

For the past few years, my family has attended several camping festivals all over the country. It's been wonderful to get outside, smell evergreen trees, and relax at a campfire with friends. This regular escape keeps us in touch with a simpler side of ourselves, an unhurried natural side. I find that just sitting outside with a good book outside, while my children play around me is a wonderfully effective de-stressor for me.

I've met a few people now who almost never wear shoes. They spend most of their time outside and in touch with the Earth directly through their feet. They say that it's the easiest way to stay "grounded" or mindfully present, and it makes sense. Being in constant contact with the planet is appealing to me. When was the last time you walked barefoot on a grassy lawn, a beach, or in the soft dirt of your garden? It feels good!

Dr. Marc Berman from the University of Michigan found that people had a 20% increase in memory and attention after only 10 minutes spent walking in an area with trees. Just looking at pictures of nature while sitting in a quiet room can give some benefit, and is significantly more useful than walking down a busy city street. Plants improve concentration and creativity. It is also well known that *real* plants are necessary for this effect. If people learn that plants are fake, they feel duped, and the positive effects are lost.

Armed with this knowledge I've transformed my parenting. There are days when the girls have their hair braided and faces washed. We still eat supper together every night and encourage proper table etiquette. But we always make time for outside play, and I do my best to have a light-hearted attitude toward mud, tangles, and dirty fingernails. The red noses, rosy cheeks, and out-of-breath screams of delight are worth those risks, and the extra time in the tub.

There is a reason many people find gardening relaxing and rewarding! Unfortunately, many of us don't make time for it until we're retired. We need to make time for nature now! And we must encourage it in our youth. Instead of sharing the meme on Facebook lamenting the loss of outdoor play for children, send your kids and grandchildren outside *now*. For that matter, get out there with them! Get a hula hoop or a jump rope and exercise. Hang a hammock and read a book with a glass of lemonade. Take your coffee outside first thing in the morning, enjoy the crisp air for a few minutes, and *dream* about the day's possibilities.

To incorporate nature into our mindfulness practice, I now encourage regular picnics for my little girls. They have a favorite spot, under the "picnic tree" where they sit and eat snack lunches. I have a large garden. The whole family loves harvesting our home-grown produce. We take walks on our property while the girls look for fairies. We open windows and allow a breeze to flow through our home. Several rooms have houseplants, and my goal is to have at least one in every room of the house.

Your mindfulness practice

Get outside! Cast aside any self-imposed shackles of cleanliness. Make time to get sunshine on your skin every day, and to bask in the beauty of this planet. Notice how resilient nature is, that weeds and grass continue to peek between sidewalk slabs and driveway cracks. See how, even in the city, wildlife surrounds you and shares your space. Taking time to notice and experience nature does us a world of good; pun intended.

Day 23: Fellowship

The following is a message I recently sent to some close friends:

Dearest neighbor,

I'm sending you this message because I adore board games! Mr. Brown, he's of a different sort. He can talk for long hours on nearly any subject (many I find only slightly interesting): creating tables from trees, car repairs, electroplating, and endless business ideas. At long last, I've decided that it is time for us to engage in some friendly game play with our fellow local humans. Men who may be inclined to discuss the current value of silver, politics, and the state of their carburetors, and ladies who enjoy discussing things of a more feminine sort (and also dragons and Thor, books and dreams and how everyone's children are faring in their studies). Indeed, we need friends and fellowship, wine and games, and YOU are invited. The first gathering is this Sunday at 2 PM, wherein we shall engage in a friendly competitive game of Settlers of Catan, eat food, and shout over our children, who will run and scream and play and watch movies and eat popcorn (possibly not in that order, and with as few bruises as possible). I shall serve up a pot of pasta with chicken, bacon, and broccoli - and you can bring anything you like that is edible or imbibable. Note *that our home is old, too small, and not at all clean enough for this venture, but we're doing it anyway. Because friendship, that's why. Kindly RSVP because Catan allows for 6 players only. If you've never played before, come anyway (I always win, even against other experienced players *insert maniacal evil laugh here*). See you soon!*

> "What is a friend? A single soul dwelling in two bodies."
> - Aristotle

> "You must remember, family is often born of blood, but it doesn't depend on blood.
> Nor is it exclusive of friendship. Family members can be your best friends, you know.
> And best friends, whether or not they are related to you, can be your family."
> - Trenton Lee Stewart, *The Mysterious Benedict Society*

I live in the rural Colorado plains. We have a quiet life without booming car stereos or emergency sirens. Our night sky is full of stars and milky way. It's idyllic and freeing. There are times, however, when it can be just a tad lonely.

Many of my friends live in far away cities or across oceans from me. It's been difficult, making friends while out on adventures, and not being able to bring any of them home with me! Being with people of like mind, with others that support your weirdness, and mix a little of their own in, is rewarding. It feels good to be appreciated, accepted, and wanted.

I do have some local friends, and they are quite dear to me. In fact, they just might get tired of my constant and continual invitations. Board games, dinner, bar-b-ques, movies, and even Maypole dances, are just a few of the gatherings I invite people over for. I adore boardgames. All of my children have been brought up to be game lovers because I'm so fond of this pastime. I enjoy the one-on-one interactions, the laughter and friendly competition. I love that we're talking and engaged with each other, instead of quietly sitting and facing a screen while watching a movie.

Have no other goal in mind than the joy of spending time together with friends and family. Play games, host potlucks, treasure hunts, and formulate holiday traditions, in order to bring communities together, and solidify familial relationships. Events like these also serve to ground you mindfully to the relationships that are most important to you.

For pre-teens and teenagers, supper time, family gatherings and traditions, and game nights serve to give them a comforting break from the pressures of society and their peers. These activities give older children an opportunity to talk openly in a safe and loving environment. It bonds teenagers to their families, and creates memories of healthy communication and problem solving. We have non-negotiable family time. Holidays, game nights, and especially daily supper time, are kept sacred by our teens. Our family is meant to be their foundation and their source for morality. We help them with answers to hard choices, the formation of their characters, and so much more! Ensuring they spend as much time as possible with us is paramount. Younger children benefit just as much from special family time and friendly gatherings. Include the whole family!

We have a fire pit in our back yard, and have had people come and camp on our property. Nothing is more stress relieving than being outside on a warm summer night around a fire, chatting and laughing, playing live music, and dancing with friends. I've heard friends complain that they were heading back to the "normal or muggle" world after leaving, which makes me feel truly grateful for our property and the quiet respite it provides to our guests.

Close, loving relationships are extremely important, in fact integral, to our happiness. Humans need routine, positive interactions with others in order to feel whole and well-balanced. Having regular fellowship reduces stress and helps us feel safe in an unpredictable world. These positive communication experiences draw our attention away from our day-to-day survival instincts, and pull us into a time of relaxed rest from stress and fear.

Happiness is contagious, and its effects are lasting. Even if you have to fake it as your guests arrive, before you know it your mood will be uplifted. The joy of fun, games, and food, will take over and heal your worries, hurt, and pain. You are *your own remedy* for sadness. Gathering with friends helps hurt fade. It's the reason you will gather together after someone passes away. You can empathize and commiserate, and work through your feelings *together*. You heal and find peace when you can say goodbye with others who feel the same sense of loss.

Gatherings for glad occasions work similarly. Weddings and births are joyous reasons to gather friends and family. These celebrations serve to memorialize the peaks of our happiness. They create intense and lasting memories of the *best* times of our lives. Sharing these moments with friends and family gives opportunity for building relationships, and the benefit of reminiscing in the future.

Couples who have regular intellectual conversations, experience new things together, and regularly uplift and support each other, have more successful relationships. The same occurs in friendships. The more you engage in *new* activities with your friends and loved ones, the stronger your relationships will be.

My husband and I decided to give our older children memories instead of presents, once they moved out of the house. On my son's 22nd birthday, we went indoor skydiving as a family. It was a thrilling experience! It served to form lasting memories for even our youngest children. The greatest benefit was the bonding of our family together, at a time when our son had moved out and was creating a life of his own. We continue to enjoy reminiscing about this happy memory, long afterward.

Spending time with friends and family is essential for building a joyful life. The care and fellowship of your neighbors can serve to bring meaning and a sense of belonging to community. I have the very best neighbors! My three closest neighbors are elderly widows. They have taught me a great deal about loss, strength, grace and beauty. On any given day they can be seen tending the irrigation in their farm fields, caring for horses, or mowing lawns. They bring us pies and cookies during the holidays and call upon us for help with snakes, fallen tree branches, and stubborn machinery. They are inquisitive and caring, but most of all they are examples of strength and beauty that fill me with respect. I'm so thankful to be surrounded by such strong women every day. It is my great joy and honor to check on them after a storm, or sneak up and hang May flowers from their doors with my children.

While these women grew up in a time quite different from my own generation, they have something important to teach about neighborliness. They never fail to deliver a home cooked meal to a family with a new baby, or after a funeral. They know how to whip up a pie at a moment's notice as a thank-you for small kindnesses, and will stop to chat for a few moments any time they see us outside as they drive by.

I've learned how to be a good neighbor from these ladies, and how to be a better friend as well. Their lessons have kept me mindfully present in my relationships, and guided me to the dying art of hand writing letters. They have taught me that a thank-you note is just as classy and valued today as it was 50 years ago, and that a personal visit with food of any kind is one of the best gifts for anyone at anytime.

I encourage you to develop deep, loving relationships with your partner, friends, and neighbors. Be mindful about your relationships. Step into the shoes of a classy, generous friend. You will find a peace there that doesn't exist elsewhere. You'll find loving reciprocation, genuine appreciation, and a deeper understanding of those people in your life. You'll also find a new part of yourself. One that is less stressed, and more joyful. You will leave a lasting legacy of family support and mentorship, and better communication for your children.

People need and crave positive human interaction, and lots

of it. You get it by cultivating relationships with people of like mind. You're automatically attracted to people who speak similarly, share your opinions, and have common interests. I often tell people who are looking for love, that - The person you are searching for is already out there, doing the activities you love and want to experience! - get out there and find them!

A loving note to my introverted readers: A good friend recently posted on facebook "I extroverted hard this weekend, so if anyone needs me I'll be in my blanket fort, coloring." I love her for that. She illustrates on a regular basis that while she enjoys getting out and having fun with friends and family, she also needs time to reflect, and recharge her batteries. Her true self is perfectly happy snacking on popcorn and watching movies in her pajamas without the pressures of social interaction. I understand and can relate to that too, so if you're one of those precious souls who is more comfortable out of the crowd than *in* it, know that getting your fellowship cup full on occasion will do you some good. Crowds and groups are optional. It only takes one friend to fill your fellowship cup!

Your mindfulness practice

Approach your acts of fellowship with friends and family as a mindful practice in joy, stress relief, and comfort. Find ways to regularly meet with people who share your passions, and bring your family together for some stress-free fun on a regular basis. Make evening meals a non-negotiable practice in family bonding.

Day 24: Animal Snuggles

"Meow." Emma called, again and again. My was she noisy today! She'd been caring for her kittens off and on, but when she wasn't with them, she roamed the house calling out and seemingly searching for something. She had called for a couple of hours before we realized she was asking us where the children were. My mother-in-law had taken the kids to her house for the day. Poor Emma was so attached to the little girls that when they were gone, she was thrown into a state of distress. I sat down and explained that the children would be back later. I petted her and gave her some much-needed attention. Though we speak different languages, she seemed to understand that everything would be alright and that the children would return in the evening. She quieted for the rest of the day, but not before warming our hearts and sending us the clear message that she reciprocates the love our daughters have for her.

"If having a soul means being able to feel love and loyalty and gratitude,
then animals are better off than a lot of humans."
- James Herriot

Since moving to the country, I've enjoyed the company of many animals. We've had cows, chickens, goats, and too many dogs and cats to mention (even a couple of runaway peahens joined us for a few days). It has been a series of adventures, with the whole family learning to care for, and play with, different kinds of animals. Even after all of those experiences, it was still exciting to hear that our outside cat, Emma, had just kindled a litter of kittens.

I couldn't bear to leave Emma outside in the cold, so we brought her inside just before the kittens were born. Having a furry pet in the house was a wonderful change for us. Emma has always followed the children around the property and watched over them as they played. She has not stopped this behavior now that she's inside. She even sleeps with them up in their loft. I've been immensely happy because I'm definitely a cat girl. Maybe it's because I'm a born lounger, channeling my inner-feline!

Sharing your home with pets can be physically and mentally beneficial, and helpful to your mindfulness practice. Pets also provide a constant source of amusement, comfort and conversation. Many friends and lovers met over a dog in the park; I assure you.

One of the biggest benefits of pet ownership is a healthier heart. You have lower blood-pressure, cholesterol, and triglycerides when you have an animal that you can regularly care for, pet and snuggle. Pets are excellent stress reducers, which lowers the risk of heart attack. In addition, pet owning heart attack patients recover faster and live longer. This is, of course, a direct link to mindfulness and peace. As you care for your pet, you feel responsible and useful. The routine developed through care of your pet keeps you mindful of your priorities throughout the day. The feeling of being needed is one of the fundamental ingredients to reducing depression.

Many animal owners get an additional benefit - exercise. Dog owners who walk their dog personally, are less likely to be obese than those who delegate this task to someone else. Equine enthusiasts who ride regularly, have similar benefits. Animals can be great personal trainers! It's a lot more difficult to say "no" to a wagging tail than it is to watch television instead of getting on the treadmill.

Many hospitals and long-term care centers use animal therapy. Animals reduce stress and anxiety, improve the cognitive abilities of dementia and Alzheimer's sufferers, and help the elderly to move more, and experience a healing child-like bliss. Animals promote faster healing and are especially effective for sick children. Pets are sensitive to human emotions, and can tell when someone needs a bit of laughter, or when they need gentle comforting instead. Even the ancient Greeks used animal therapy, bringing patients with low morale, gout, and neurological disorders, to horse ranches for treatment.

Troubled teens may benefit the most from animal therapy. A pet will give them someone to talk to when they feel they can't communicate well with the people around them. They can feel a sense of attachment to a loving entity, something that will love them back unconditionally. Being responsible for a pet's care makes a teenager an essential member of the family, promoting a sense of belonging. At a time when emotions are their strongest, and stress is high, an animal companion can be invaluable for a healthy mental outlook.

Families even benefit when a pet passes away. Children who go through the grief of losing a pet will be less traumatized by the loss of a human family member. The anxiety felt when a pet is ill can help a child develop empathy toward people with disabilities or illnesses. When I was a little girl, our family had a cat with a litter of four kittens. Just a few days after their kindling, she was hit by a car and died. I remember feeling devastated by her loss, and especially the thought that her kittens wouldn't make it without her. Our family was able to obtain special kitten formula and tiny bottles from a veterinarian. I fed the kittens and learned to care for them. It became my mission to raise the babies and teach them all they needed to know, which helped me overcome my grief for the loss of my pet.

Animal husbandry is a wonderful skill for a child to learn. As kids grow, they need to feel important and appreciated. Caring for an animal, and having the family value their efforts, can boost a child's self-esteem. The gift of a pet shows a child that you care about their well-being and happiness. It sends a signal that the desires they have to care for something, are natural and beneficial to their emotional health. Also, children who have pets or are exposed to animals early on have as much as a 33% decrease in the likelihood of allergies or eczema.

Our Emma, who was a surprise visitor of unknown origin, had a litter of seven kittens. Her babies are beautiful bundles of fur and mewling. I can't begin to tell you how happy this makes my three little girls, and of course, the little girl inside of me. Our daughters are learning to be gentle with them, to understand why their mommy may need to hide them from us if she feels they're threatened. The children are benefiting from lessons in anatomy and reproduction, and learning why our home might not be big enough for our family and eight cats! We're preparing them early for the eventuality that we'll need to find homes for them. Until that day comes, we'll all benefit from reduced stress, a boost in our happiness hormones serotonin and dopamine, and our hearts will be healthier. Our children will get a healthy dose of immune system support, and some wonderful memories to take with them wherever they go.

Having a pet may be a key ingredient in your recipe for happiness. They do so much for us, and our care for them is extremely rewarding! Responsible pet care is essential, so you must be mindful about animal selection and husbandry. These benefits occur with pets that you can hold, pet, or ride, but pets that are kept in cages or aquariums and never held don't have the same benefits. With that in mind, you can be assured that their presence alone will bring you immense joy. Pet owners are happier, live longer, and have numerous psychological benefits that those without pets do not have.

Know thyself: if for any reason the idea or experience of having a pet makes you uncomfortable, stressed, or induces any kind of allergic reaction, don't do it! Whilst pet ownership is healthy and beneficial for the majority of the population, there are people for whom it is contraindicated.

Your mindfulness practice

The next time you're considering a pet, take a look at those furry friends in your local shelter. Know that while you are giving them a home, a warm place to sleep, and some good food and hugs; they will be giving you a world of good right back. You'll have lower stress, a boost to your happy hormones, a healthier heart, and less anxiety. You'll have something to care for, and the dependency they'll have on you will help you feel needed and reduce depression. Your pet's love and intuitive support will be a boon, and you'll be mindfully returning the favor.

Day 25: The Winds of Change

She closed her eyes and turned her face toward the sun. The wind blew her curls behind her ears, and for a moment, she wondered about the state of her hair once she reached her destination. It was an hour's ride to the bookstore, long enough to tangle even the most well-conditioned locks when riding a motorcycle. She looked down at the bike. A shiny metallic red, it glistened in the sunshine. She took a deep breath of appreciation. No matter how badly tangled her hair would be in the end, she always felt empowered and free when riding. The woman reached up and began braiding her curls back, then tied the end of her brunette coif. She wrapped a folded bandanna just over her bangs and tied it securely under the braid in the back. She revved the engine, smiled and took off into the wind, heading West.

"The art of life lies in a constant
readjustment to your surroundings."
- Kakuzo Okakaura

"A wise man adapts himself to circumstances,
as water shapes itself into the vessel
that contains it."
- Chinese Proverb

I always loved the comic, Rose is Rose by Pat Brady. Especially as I got older, I appreciated the young, tired mother who looked into store windows and imagined herself as a fierce, curly-haired biker chick. She reminded me of myself, poised when meeting new people, every bit the mother, wife, and friend I should be, with inner thoughts of dragon slaying, motorcycle riding, and skydiving, a part of my daily imaginings. *Wind in my hair… don't care!*

The wind plays an integral role in our planet's weather system. Air moves around our planet, absorbing energy from the sun and moving much-needed moisture. It brings life-giving oxygen to the beasts and carbon dioxide to the plants. In its travels it picks up dust and debris from the surface of the Earth and moves it around, contributing to seed spreading and pollination. In the course of human history, many different societies have created myths and legends regarding the air and the wind, and its importance in our lives.

There are over fifty references to deities named for wind and air movement. Many religious texts mention the wind as divine, holy, or a gift from the divine. There are numerous wives tales, mythological stories, and folklore related to the wind. The "winds of change" is a common phrase, used in songs and superstitions alike.

Growing up in Eastern Colorado, I've always had to contend with wind. Aside from a short three-year stint in Southern California, I've rarely seen calm days that resulted in perfect hair lasting until afternoon. Long before "beach hair" became popular, we mountain girls were rocking the slightly messy hair look, with a little help from mother nature.

When you grow up around the wind, you become accustomed to it. You step out of your door, close your eyes, and greet the breeze as one might an old friend. Our children track the weather throughout the year, and nearly every day is recorded as windy on their monthly charts. I'd like to share with you one of the most helpful mindfulness lessons I've ever learned - embrace the wind, and embrace **change**.

We spend too much of our lives fighting change, and complaining about things that are completely out of our control. The wind is definitely on that list. When was the last time you walked outside on a windy day and just embraced it? Just ran out into that crazy wind and let it buffet you and push you in the direction of its choosing? What would it feel like if you did that? Do you think you'd feel a bit out of control? A little crazy, and a little free-spirited?

Mindful thoughts regarding change are similar to our response to strong wind. Initially, you fight it and complain. Then you resign yourself to it (because as reluctant as we may be, the wind/change is there and it's not going away). Lastly, you accept the wind (and the change) and move forward. You slowly realize everything will be OK. The sun will still rise tomorrow, just like it always has.

I remember getting my first gray hair. I know it's a cliche', but I was horrified. I thought I'd have many more years before gray hair became a part of me, but there it was, right in the middle of my part line. It practically screamed its existence at me in the mirror. I pulled that sucker out before I even knew what I was doing. I was amazed that it had gone unnoticed for so long. The next thing I knew I was setting up an appointment for an age-defying tattoo.

After I had a couple of weeks to think things through (and notice two or three more conspiratorial hairs), I realized they weren't so bad. Firstly, I called my mom to ask her when she started getting the dreaded grays and discovered that it was right about the same time that I had. I briefly chastised her for not giving me a proper warning, but then we both laughed about it. Secondly, I vowed never to hesitate to share my age, and to embrace the process of aging. Revlon may (or may not) be a part of my "process".

As I age I learn more and more about change, why we initially fight it, and how to be mindful in the face of it. It's always my goal to be graceful during changes, as I watch my children grow out of diapers and into driver's licenses. Somehow I end up shedding more tears than I'd planned, or holding onto the past a little longer and harder than I expected. I've learned that this is perfectly natural too.

My eldest daughter recently finished school and moved to the city. Things didn't work out well for her. After a short time there, and a bit of heartache, she came home for a cry session and to ask for advice. I invited her to move back in and save money, the advice I thought was in her best interest. She immediately had the offer to stay with her father in the city, to live with him for the first time, and get to know him better. She would also be able to continue her career where there are better opportunities. I realized that my offer had really been quite selfish. It was an attempt to hold onto her a little longer and preserve some of the little girl she'd been. It was unfair of me, and if she'd accepted, I would have held her back. As soon as I learned of her father's offer, I encouraged her to take the opportunity, realizing it was far better for her.

While it takes a great deal of practice and patience to accept change in our lives, it can be far more peaceful than resisting it. The serenity poem/prayer encourages us to notice the difference between things we cannot change and things we can. You already have the answer, but sometimes it helps to ask yourself if this is a situation that *you can change*. If not, you can let it go and move on. You cannot halt your children from growing up, or your parents from aging. You can't stop the gray hairs from coming.

The winds of change will come. When they do, choose to mindfully accept them. You can allow them to blow through and tangle your hair and your life. As you work through those tangles, you grow and gain wisdom to help the next generation through the same processes. Like us, they may need time (sometimes years) to hear our advice and learn to let go. That's OK too - we each have our process and our path, which can only be chosen by us.

Embracing your path is a prelude to accepting the journey of others. You cannot choose their path for them, make their choices, or protect them from pain. What you *can* do, is grow as mindfully wise as you can, share advice and love when it's asked for, and allow the wind to bring with it what it will. Gratitude helps us focus on joy during this never-ending process. It keeps us grounded to what is truly important.

Your mindfulness practice

You may plan for your life's journey from point A to point B in a straight line, but life is full of unexpected twists and turns. Step into your greatness! Let the winds come, and bring their change with them! We shall be strong as rocks on the shore, mindful of our gratitude, and full of love and peace.

Day 26: Flowing Waters

I walked along the path slowly, my heart racing. It was just around the corner. A sacred space millions had visited before me, and had been blessed, married, christened. I took small steps, my breath coming in short gasps, tears welling up as I got closer. I'd already seen the other signs and symbols in the gardens - the vesica pool, the lion's head spout where I drank my first sip of the healing waters. I passed a small statued alcove and saw the final stone archway. As I entered the small enclosure around the sacred well, tears flowed freely, and I gasped with emotion. I felt my heart swell with fear, joy, and excitement as I gazed down on the metal-inlay well head. This sacred place that I'd only read about became suddenly real for me. I was standing where so many had stood before, gazing down at a natural wonder. The Chalice Well was just as beautiful and magical as I'd hoped. I sat there for almost an hour, praying, weeping, and contemplating as the sun rose and illuminated the well-kept gardens. For the rest of my life, I know that this place, and the energy I felt while there, will be with me as a calming reminder of renewal and hope.

"Let the rain kiss you.
Let the rain beat upon your head

with silver liquid drops.
Let the rain sing you a lullaby."
- Langston Hughes

"So let the mind flow like water.
Face life with a calm and quiet mind
and everything in life will be
calm and quiet."
- Thich Thien-An

I am fascinated by the beauty and history of the Chalice Well. I traveled to Glastonbury, England in 2010 and made my pilgrimage to the gardens and both the red and white wells. I had learned years earlier; that ancient wells were seen as gifts from the Gods, divine healing waters that mysteriously never dried up. Those two wells, in particular, have wonderful mythological tales associated with them, and religious significance for people of many faiths. The waters are vastly different in mineral content, even though the springs flow just feet apart and come from the same ancient source at the base of the Glastonbury Tor.

Water is necessary for life. It is cleansing and creating, but it can also be destructive. Our world wouldn't be the same without it, and one of the foremost goals of our space program is to find more of it on other worlds. Water is always moving, flowing, falling. It nourishes our body and the land around us. Water evokes feelings of happiness and satisfaction, calm, peace, and unity.

Being near water calms your mind and gives you a much-needed rest from the over stimulation of our modern society. Water focuses your thoughts with a rhythm and gentle flow that is meditative. Being near water helps you to focus and dial in your thoughts so that you can better concentrate. Water pushes out other distractions. The ancient Romans had bathhouses all over their cities to entertain, calm, and cleanse the stresses of the day away from their patrons.

Since water does such a good job of distracting people, it enhances meditation. Listening to ocean waves, babbling brooks, or the rhythmic dripping of a rain shower is a method for attaining a meditative state quickly. Often these sounds will help you sleep, reduce stress, and calm anxiety. While many experts will encourage you to "ground" when we're stressed or anxious, you may be better served by "watering" instead!

Our planet is called "Big Blue" by many astronauts and NASA employees. Seen from space, our planet is mostly water-covered, and thus appears cerulean. She is stunningly beautiful! Upon returning home, astronauts speak of the spiritual experiences they've had while in space. Most have a greater sense of connection to all of humanity, and a loss of interest in politics and petty disagreements. They have seen the entire planet, and how tiny we are compared to the vastness of space. The blue waters of our lakes and oceans called to them from miles above the surface, calmed their internal dialogues, and reminded them of their source - that which is most important - their *humanity*.

Water increases creativity and problem solving as well. Ask anyone who's wished they had a waterproof notepad in the shower! Some of the best ideas of our time have come to people while bathing. The ancient Greek scholar Archimedes exclaimed "Eureka! Eureka!" from his bathtub as he made a discovery regarding water displacement. The "eureka effect" is the common human experience of remembering something or understanding a previous problem. Scientists say that our brains work best at solving problems when we have dopamine flowing, are relaxed, and distracted. Showers, hot tubs, and dips in quiet pools do all those things for us.

Because of water's remarkable benefits, adding a water feature near you at just about any time, will reduce your stress and improve your mood and concentration. Exercising in or near water helps you work out in a more rhythmic fashion. It reduces tension in the muscles, which can help reduce injury. A water feature in your workspace makes you more creative, helps your mind solve problems, inspires you, and uplifts your mood while you work. Water features help reduce stress in the home, helping people communicate better, reducing conflict, and uplifting everyone's moods.

Water is prominently featured in many religious contexts as well. It's used for ritual purification and cleansing, and to prepare oneself for prayer or entering holy buildings. Many religions build temples near water for this purpose. Ancient peoples from all over the world, regardless of religion, used water as a method for purifying themselves for worship or sending messages directly to the divine.

With our bodies being more than 60% water, it is no wonder that water has so much influence on our minds and our spiritual practices. The moon's cycles affect not only our planet but quite possibly our bodies as well. Many women purport susceptibility to the phases of the moon, and its distance from the Earth. With this understanding, how then might you use water in your mindfulness practice?

In the ancient art of Feng Shui, water is one of the most important elements to consider around your home or office. The words Feng Shui translate to "wind and water". In this practice, water is seen as representing flow, prosperity, and abundance. It is important that energy flows into and out of your home through natural pathways. Feng Shui teaches that water features and water symbolism can be used to achieve that. By adding a water feature to your front entrance, for example, prosperity and abundance are said to "flow" into your home or office.

As you go through your life and notice the flow of daily energy, you can chart a graph of your feelings, energy, and emotions that (for women at least) can be quite predictable. There are days you struggle to find energy and motivation, days where your energy and motivation are powerfully strong, and days that are contemplative, fierce, or melancholy. During those times when you are out of focus or lost, being near water can boost your mood and your mindful approach to life.

Water can help you return to a state of focus upon your priorities and your goals. Its meditative nature can allow you to shut out all distractions, and bring your goals back into the forefront of your consciousness. Water allows you to cleanse your mind and create the natural flow of creativity and problem solving that is innate in your subconscious. A bath or shower is all it takes to find that state of calm concentration and promote creative thinking.

Slow down as you wash your hands, and focus on the water

flowing over your skin. Feel the temperature of the water, and imagine its source. Draw upon the energy of that place deep within the Earth that the water may have come from, or high up in the sky where the water cycle refreshed it so it could rain down again on the planet. Take the strength and energy of those places with you, as you go about your tasks. The next time it rains, dance and play in the water falling from the sky. This small, playful ritual is one of the most mood uplifting activities that I can think of. I'm never left frowning after a dance in the rain! If your significant other is with you, be sure to steal a kiss! Give them the benefit of a rain dance as well, and a boost to your dopamine and serotonin levels with a romantic smooch!

Your mindfulness practice

Water is a guide toward focused calm. Use it regularly in your mindfulness practice. Flowing water can be enjoyed in your home, and you probably live near natural water. Spend time in quiet contemplation near water when you can. Practice gratitude for the clean, clear water available to you while enjoying its many benefits.

Day 27: Crawlies Aren't All Creepy

I was making popcorn. The kids were in bed. Danger and I were just settling down to watch a film together. I bent over to get the popcorn pan from the bottom cabinet under the counters and thought I saw a mouse out of the corner of my eye. We live in the country, surrounded by grain farms, and mice are a regular nuisance. I turned to look and opened my mouth to tell Danger to set another mousetrap when I saw ***it****. My brain (more specifically, my amygdala) registered the arachnid before the rest of me. In true comic style, I leaped up about three feet into the air, twisted my body and ran across the kitchen. I jumped up onto the counter and sat whimpering, unable to utter a proper word. My poor, worried husband quickly ran to my aid and saw the offender at once. He uttered a single "Whoa!" and turned to grab a flyswatter to dispatch it. Meanwhile, two curious little girls had come out of their rooms to see what all the hubbub was about. I tried to shoo them away in my panic, which was slowly receding. After he had killed the giant spider, he turned to me, and with eyes full of sympathy, said he would have thought it was a mouse too…a large mouse! He came and held me until I felt able to climb down from the counter.*

"The oldest and strongest emotion of mankind is fear."
- H.P. Lovecraft

"When you explore your fears then you set yourself free."
- Stephen Richards, *Releasing You From Fear*

This was not my first experience with fight or flight. It was actually the third time, all three being initiated by an eight-legged visitor. My mother is certainly to blame for my fear of spiders - as she has the same issue with these little creepy-crawlies. You can say that it runs in the family, but I've been working with diligence for years to rid myself of this debilitation.

And it IS debilitating. Irrational fears are a problem, an irritation, or at the very least, embarrassing. I often imagine what my life would be like if I didn't have this phobia. What would it be like if I could replace my fear with curiosity? I've read all about fear elimination. Everything from hypnotherapy to shocking Fear Factor immersion training, to EFT (Emotional Freedom Technique) and counseling. Many of these methods sounded unappealing to me. My goal wasn't to have a tarantula walking on my arm. I just didn't want to panic and lose control of my body every time a spider showed its legs unexpectedly.

It turns out that one of the best ways to get rid of a phobia is to educate yourself. Being a person who enjoys continual self-education, I decided that I would begin learning about spiders. In the beginning, I disabled images in my browser as I read online. Even a photo of a spider could send me into a panic. If you've ever seen a picture of a bird-eating tarantula, you'll see why I elected to read picture-free.

The first thing I learned was that Cellar spiders, or "Daddy Long Legs" (not even spiders, the leggy rascals) as we call them here in Colorado, are actually quite friendly and work to keep your home free from other bug pests, including other spiders that are not so friendly. That bit of knowledge was reassuring and comforting. After learning more about them, I'm comfortable with those creatures. I have to clean up after them all the time because they leave their messy webs all over my ceiling, but at least they're not interested in eating me.

Next, I thought I'd learn about wolf spiders. It turns out that the biggun' that was in my kitchen posing as a mouse was a wolf spider. These spiders also hunt other insects, even the awful grasshoppers that decimate my garden, and tiny mice. I was surprised that they almost never harm humans, although their bite is venomous. Like most spiders, they only bite people when provoked, and prefer tinier prey. Knowing more about them has changed me completely. Instead of fear, I have some respect. Instead of wanting to smash them all, I am comfortable with relocating them outside.

While we do have some spiders in our area that *are* dangerous (black widow, brown recluse), I've learned that most spiders pretty much ignore us. They are just not at all interested in people. They don't care about our TV shows, our family drama, or our exercise plan. They're not interested in our petty gossip about the neighbor lady, and they are only interested in our garden because there are other bugs there - bugs they actually want to socialize with (aka munch on).

I have three young daughters. It is imperative to me that I avoid imparting this phobia of spiders to them. While educating myself about spiders, I'm sharing all the information with my girls as well. As a family, we encourage daddy to catch and release, as opposed to black-belt karate squishing.

The Buddhists believe that all life is sacred, even the smallest insect. I certainly agree with them that all life has purpose. I'm learning to be mindful regarding my fear, and to be more rational and educated about the creatures I come in contact with. While it's only natural for our brain's amygdala to jump in like a knight on a dark bridge to say "Halt! Who goes there?!" anytime it feels threatened, it's also nice to be able to pat Stallone brain on the bicep and say, "It's OK, big guy, he's with me." and not immediately jump to running away or squishing.

I have friends with similar irrational fears toward spiders, snakes, mice, dogs, birds, and other misunderstood creatures of the world. I've succeeded in recommending to a few that they educate themselves about these creatures, to improve their reaction to them. As you strive to live a meaningful joy-filled life, fear can get in the way. Conquering your fears empowers you to enjoy life as you were meant to!

My husband and I first met at a 911 dispatchers continuation training course. The class was held in a secure government building, underground. During the class, a coworker who had traveled to take the class with me nudged my arm. She pointed for me to look to my left, where an immense spider was enjoying the lecture from astride a cardboard box. No one in the classroom expected my reaction, least of all me. While wearing a skirt, I leaped out of my chair and sprang over the rear two rows of students! I ran at top speed out of the room, and up the stairs to the exit. The exit was electronically controlled by the dispatchers, who had no idea that someone was at the door hoping to flee for their lives, so I was stuck in the bunker. I don't know how long I stood at the top of the stairs trying to open the door until one of the other students came to check on me. The class of 20 people was given a break, and I was nearly catatonic with fear. When I finally came back into the room, there was an awkward silence. Young Mr. Brown looked at me and said, for all the crowd to hear, "Don't be embarrassed, I feel the same way about commitment!" which broke the ice. We were all able to laugh about it and move on.

It was the most embarrassing thing that has ever happened to me. And I had absolutely no control over my actions! I'm sharing it with you because since that time I've not only learned to control my fear, and overcome a good portion of it but I've become far more mindful and at peace when it comes to animals and insects that once caused me trepidation. This mindful awareness of my fear, and action to educate myself has done wonders for me. I'm free from that pain and torment.

I used to spend the last few minutes before going to bed looking for spiders. I looked for spiders whenever I entered a new room, and when I later got a job answering the 911 emergency line in that same bunker, I often searched the facility for spiders before and during my shift. It was such a waste of energy, and all that fear only served to diminish my joy. I am so thankful for the time I've spent educating myself about these truly interesting creatures! I've gained a healthy respect and admiration for them and released a part of myself that wasn't good for me.

Your Mindfulness Practice

About 4%-5% of the population have phobias similar to the one I suffered with. But many more people (especially women) suffer from anxiety and fears that might be helped with mindful self-education. If you feel fearful or anxious regarding a certain situation, educating yourself about that situation can help immensely. As you learn, you become more confident and empowered. Taking control of your fears makes more room for serenity and merriment in your life.

Day 28: A cuppa

I handed the bottle to the person on my left. He poured a bit into his glass and passed it around to others sitting around the campfire. The fire crackled and popped as the bottle went to each person in turn. As they took their first sips, I heard tiny moans of pleasure escape their lips. Unbeknownst to me, I'd stumbled into the Orpheus camp, a chamber choir that hosted a well-known mead gathering and contest every year. Mead is a fermented honey wine, usually home brewed and flavored with fruits or spices. We were at Beltania, a camping event in Colorado where families came to celebrate May Day, dance the May pole dance, and fellowship and frolic, to celebrate the coming of spring. They all praised my first mead, and before I left their camp I was made to feel like a star. Later, my mead was called a "true potion," a delight for the senses, and a sure winner for a mead "cup" or contest for amateur brewers. I walked from camp to camp sharing my mead well into the night, enjoying the company of strangers, stars, and firelight.

"I say let the world go to hell,
but I should always have my tea."
- Fyodor Dostoyevsky

"I have measured out my life with coffee spoons."
- T. S. Elliot

Your body is over 60% water, and you must continually drink more to keep your body functioning well. Like many other things, not only does it benefit you to mindfully explore how and what you drink, but it can improve your mood and prevent overindulgences if you drink with a mindful attitude.

I'm a morning coffee drinker. I take out one of my favorite Dutch mugs and make a small pot of half-caf in my French press. While my kettle heats, I determine my focus for the day and say some affirmations. After my coffee is poured and the cream stirred in, I walk to a big picture window in my dining room. Relishing the aroma, gazing out at the landscape, I take my first sip. I admire the view of the farm field across the dirt road and wish safe travels for the early morning truck drivers passing by. This is a time for me to send loving thoughts to friends and family, and think of those who have shared concerns with me.

I drink my coffee slowly and use it as a meditation in gratitude. The warmth of the liquid is a comfort, and I look forward to the enjoyable pick-me-up. I dilute my coffee grounds by half with Teeccino, to reduce my caffeine intake. However, there's still plenty to jump start my day. For nearly eight years I was caffeine-free, because I was pregnant or nursing my infants during that time. I didn't want my babies to have any caffeine in their little systems. I'm happy to drink it again now that the children are no longer depending on my body for nourishment.

I stopped drinking soda of any kind in 2005. Gestational diabetes led me to research a healthier diet. While sugar and chemicals are excellent reasons to stop drinking soda, I found the idea of drinking our calories to be far more convincing. Food is fuel for our bodies. Everything you ingest contributes to your health or disease. By drinking something with a lot of sugar or calories, you're gaining weight without getting the benefit of a full tummy and nourishment. No, thank you!

Fall and winter afternoons mean tea in the Brown household. While the children are especially fond of chamomile, my husband and I drink Builders Black, green, or one of my herbal tea mixtures. I dehydrate fruit and herbs that I grow or find on sale, and often create my own herbal tea blends. It is a rewarding experience to serve homemade herbal tea to a guest or a stressed family member. I love to watch them relax and see their tension melt away. Every cup has a special ingredient - **love**.

My favorite fall activity is to sit in a quiet room with a good book and a cup of tea. And there's no substitute for a cool summer morning, on the porch with my coffee. We often see pictures of people on porches in the summer, with glasses of iced tea, and smiles on their faces. Or, better yet, those luxurious images of pillowed hammocks and lemonade. Whether the liquid is hot or cold, we often associate comfort with drinking.

I've found that by focusing wholly on whatever may be in my glass, I can relax and refill my internal "cup" as well. While breaking from hard work in the garden on a hot day, a glass of iced water, tea, or lemonade is refreshing. It brings to mind the indulgence of jumping into a swimming pool or swinging on a rope into a chilly river. A good book, snuggling in front of a crackling fireplace, and holiday laughter are all brought to mind when drinking a hot beverage.

When you're struggling with stress and feeling overwhelmed, being present with your beverage slows you down. The memories and images evoked by the drink can heal your day. Mindfulness expert Eckhart Tolle once said, "Just drink your tea!". Focus on the tea and nothing else at all. Let all your worries, regrets, and any other distractions, just slip away. Simply drink your tea, nothing else.

You can do this meditation practice with any drink. Focus on where the ingredients came from, the beautiful mountain source of the pure water, and either the refreshment of the cool drink or the luxury of a hot beverage. Let it flow deep into your body, to your bones, and fill your emotional "cup". Focus on the good feelings that a pleasant drink gives you.

Water is extremely important for every bodily system. Dehydration can cause memory loss, depression, kidney disease, cramps and sore muscles. Being mindful about our water intake is essential for our well-being. Your body will tell you when you are dehydrated. Your countenance drops and your head begins to ache. You'll lose patience with others and with yourself. Being sensitive to dehydration will make you more aware of it, especially since you don't start to feel thirsty until your body is already dehydrated!

Since the effects of dehydration are so significant, you'd think that we would all be naturally aware of our hydration levels, and seek to keep our bodies well-hydrated. This isn't so, however. For most of us, hydration doesn't cross our mind at all during the day, and if we start to feel sluggish, cranky, or get a headache, dehydration is rarely our first suspect. Interestingly, we begin to feel thirsty after losing only 1%-2% of our body's water supply.

Every time you drink water, your body thanks you! It thanks you with glowing skin, tears, joint lubrication, and focused thought. Your body has carried you all through your life so far, with whatever level of hydration you've provided. You're reading this text, and your body isn't protesting your lack of hydration with any kind of banners, rallies, or picket signs. Should it be? Are you well-hydrated? Do you drink a glass of water when you first wake, knowing that you are most dehydrated after a night's rest? Do you alternate water and alcoholic beverages, knowing that alcohol dehydrates you and is a diuretic, working to flush additional liquid from your body? The biggest factor in the creation of a hangover is dehydration and loss of electrolytes. Drink!

Keeping yourself hydrated has other, compounding benefits. If you sit at a desk during the day, being well hydrated forces you to get up on a regular basis to head to the restroom! This also means that your eyes get a much-needed rest from the computer screen, and your body can stretch. Taking a short walk every 30 minutes can also give you a burst of creativity and energy, increasing your work performance.

Alcohol is a tender subject. No one wants to be told how they should live their life. As adults, we don't wish for someone to point an accusing finger in our direction and attack us for our behavior. I feel that the consumption of alcohol is a personal choice, especially since it has such religious and cultural significance. I personally resonate with the Buddhist view on alcohol. I feel it is important for me to make wise choices, and be a voice of wisdom to my children, friends, and family. For this reason, I limit my alcohol consumption. I do not impair my ability to speak with wisdom. I drink the occasional glass of red wine, or home-brewed mead, refraining from drunkenness.

More and more, I find myself abstaining from alcohol due to its dramatic effect on brain function for up to 48 hours after drinking. As I develop my coaching practice, speaking and writing business, I need all the focus and concentration that my mind can give me. By choosing not to drink, I'm able to perform at my best for the people who need me.

My husband is a teetotaler. A close family friend lost his wife to cirrhosis of the liver, and my husband has been humbly sober ever since. I admire and support his decision fully. Whatever your choices regarding alcohol consumption, I recommend that you imbibe safely, carefully, and with intention. Being mindful about your drinking will add additional purpose to your life, better flesh out your personal credo, and lead to increased joy.

Your mindfulness practice

At least once per day, focus all your thought on your drinking. Whether your choice is something hot or cool, or just plain water, simply enjoy the process of drinking and embrace the images, feelings, and memories that your drink brings. Be mindful of your water intake, and care for your body by keeping your fluid levels high.

Day 29: A Good Meal

I finished whisking the ganache and brought it to the counter. Very slowly, I poured it in long streaks across my double-layered chocolate cheesecake. It was huge, the biggest cheesecake I'd ever seen, and absolutely gorgeous. When I finished, there were four layers: A dark chocolate pressed cookie crust, a pure white cheesecake, a chocolate mousse, and finally the dark chocolate ganache drizzled over the whole thing. It had taken me two days of preparation and cooking to create. After snapping a picture and receiving "oohs and ahhs" as accolades from my family and friends, I cut into my creation and began serving slices. The guests could not wait for me to finish serving, and I was delighted to hear giggles, mmm's and other exclamations of pleasure as everyone took their first bite. When I finally got my piece, it was so rich and decadent, that one bite could have completely satisfied me. I ate deliberately, savoring each layer, and enjoying the reward of my hard work. It was magnificent!

"One cannot think well, love well, sleep well,
if one has not dined well."
- Virginia Woolf

"When walking, walk.
When eating, eat."
- Rashaski Zen Proverb

As I write this chapter on mindful eating, I'm planning our Thanksgiving gathering. I'm taking into consideration invitations I've sent and received, and the dietary restrictions and individual preferences for my guests. I'm also pondering decor, the size of my dining table and number of chairs I own, games we could play, and how to entertain the children. It didn't take long for there to be some miscommunication and hurt feelings, which has reminded me that we should not only eat mindfully, but plan our meals with mindfulness.

Danger and I have changed our day-to-day eating habits dramatically since we first got together. What was once simply an afterthought has become a major focus for us, ethically, politically, and medically. Throughout all of our dietary changes, however, we have learned that our political opinion regarding food should never be the focus of a gathering, make meals complicated, or prevent them from happening altogether.

We have many friends that do not share our views regarding food, much less our personal diets when we're working to improve our health. It would be highly inappropriate for us to force our friends to eat a limited diet just for the sake of a single gathering. We don't ask our friends not to drink soda, just because we've chosen not to drink it. We would never ask our friends or family not to serve hot dogs, shrimp, or crab because we've decided not to consume those things. We just let it go.

We enjoy potlucks, suppers with friends, restaurants, meals on special occasions, and holiday feasts, with much abandon. Food is filled with incredibly personal choices regarding sustainability, health, bycatch concerns, and other issues. Why would we ignore those things just because we happen to be dining with friends or family? Because food is social.

We often use food as an excuse to gather in groups. We invite people over for supper, out for a cup of coffee, or to gather for holiday meals. During this time, it's more important to enjoy company, to be gracious and grateful for the time with these cherished people, than it is to impose our food preferences. We teach our children to take a bite of everything they're offered, to always be graciously thankful, even when they're served something that isn't their first preference.

Since allergies can be life threatening (my eldest daughter has a shellfish allergy), they are the one exception to this particular practice. We always ask if shellfish will be served, and make organizers aware of her allergy ahead of time so she will have safe food options. If some foods create discomfort or pose a risk of any kind, you should speak up! In my experience friends and family understand these issues and accommodate them as best they can, or are very understanding if you have to bring your own food in order to be safe. I have a good friend with a severe gluten allergy. While I'd love to prepare my gluten-free brownies for her, it's just too risky for her to even try them given that I also bake wheat bread in the same kitchen. It only takes a tiny amount to cause a horrible reaction for her, so I would never bemoan her choice to bring her own food when she visits.

When eating mindfully, whether in a group or alone, the first thing you must do is slow down. People are accustomed to eating too much, too quickly. Restaurants regularly serve massive portions or encourage you to "super size" your meal. Then they do their best to get you done and out for the next round of customers, as quickly as possible. We must not allow our homes to be the same.

Have you ever seen a film wherein a Victorian family dines together? In their crisp, pristine dress, they eat slowly, between sips of wine. They discuss the day, the goings-on in the community, and letters they've received. Supper is a family affair that is rather formal, but also deliberate and slow. There is no rush here, no cell phones, and no television playing in the background.

Slow down when you eat your food. Especially when taking the very first bite. Savor it as much as possible. Ask yourself "What am I experiencing?" Enjoy the scents, the way the food looks, and how it is presented. Luxuriate in the flavor and note the textures you experience. This practice will help you to enjoy your food, and experience it in new ways. Is there a flavor that surprises you, or a taste that you've never experienced before? Does your friend make her meatloaf a little differently? While eating can you pinpoint the ingredients she uses, without asking her?

Next, we'll focus on where the meal came from. How can you demonstrate your appreciation for the food preparer? The animal the meat comes from? The garden or farm where the produce was grown? You can experience gratitude for where your food came from. Let the cook know you appreciate the meal if you enjoyed it. Don't hesitate to ask a waitress to tell the kitchen staff if a meal was particularly well made. In our family, we always teach our children to thank a host or hostess for the meal and to appreciate the food they eat. We also wait until the cook takes the first bite before we eat, out of courtesy.

When mindfulness becomes a part of your day-to-day experience, start to notice things that you may have missed before. You may notice eating habits that are unnecessary, or are a result of stress or feeling down. To avoid consuming unnecessary calories, ask yourself "Am I really hungry?", before grabbing a snack. In addition, you may find that you are completely satisfied after drinking a glass of water. Dehydration often feels similar to hunger.

If you are able to be a bit mindful whilst eating, you will benefit from the peace and satisfaction it brings to your meal. If you catch yourself eating quickly or forgetting your interest in mindful eating, that's OK. Not every bite has to be mindful, for you to have the benefit of gratitude and appreciation for your meal. And while your friends and family probably already know that you appreciate their hospitality, say so anyway. It certainly feels good to hear it! It is polite to let them know that you've enjoyed their home, their food, and their company. Better yet, surprise them with a classy, hand-written thank-you sent through the mail!

Your mindfulness practice

Slow down. Experience all the sensations your food provides. Enjoy every bite. Being a bit lax on your dietary requirements while dining with friends or attending a potluck will help you focus on fellowship. Slowing down while eating helps you appreciate your food, and recognize things you may often take for granted; like the scents, flavors, and textures of your meal. When you express gratitude, whether inwardly or outwardly, for the host/hostess, chef, garden, and animals you consume, you are bringing joy to your meal, and those responsible for putting it on your plate.

Day 30: The Healing Power of Touch

I heard her crying and ran to the kids' room. There she was, sitting on the floor, weeping over her shoes. I sat down with her and told her everything would be OK. As soon as we could, we'd go to the store and purchase new shoes for her. It's not that they didn't fit, or that she didn't like the color. They just overwhelmed her, like so many other things. She can't wear socks because of the tiny strings or seams inside that touch her toes. Even after spending extra money on seamless socks, it wasn't enough. Half of the foods she tries to eat have strange textures that she can't abide. Clothing must have tags removed before she'll consider wearing it. We even had to cut the sleeves off several shirts, so that she could stand to wear them for more than a few minutes. She wasn't allowed to ride her new bicycle for awhile because she refused to wear her bicycle helmet. The helmet strap was too uncomfortable. Eventually, we solved the problem by wrapping some soft fabric over the clasp.

This is what it's like living with a child with sensitivity issues. As I sat there on the floor with her, cajoling her into her socks and shoes so she could go to the park with grandma, she climbed into my lap and held onto me and let me stroke her hair and hug her. So many things in this world are uncomfortable for her, but she craves human contact. She comes up to me for a comforting hug several times a day, even more than she did when she was a toddler. She is one of the most intimate children I've had, snuggling for movies and book reading, and constantly expressing how good it feels when someone has their arms around her. She can't wear socks, but she can wear hugs!

> "Too often we underestimate the power of a touch,
> a smile, a kind word, a listening ear, an honest compliment,
> or the smallest act of caring, all of which have
> the potential to turn a life around."
> - Leo Buscaglia

> "I will not play tug o' war. I'd rather play hug o' war.
> Where everyone hugs instead of tugs,
> where everyone giggles and rolls on the rug,
> where everyone kisses, and everyone grins,
> and everyone cuddles and everyone wins."
> - Shel Silverstein

Human touch is amazing. We benefit incredibly from physical contact with other people. Human touch causes a decrease in violence, improves trust, cooperation, and teamwork; and increases intimacy. Our health, happiness, and wellbeing improve when we're regularly touched by another person. It comforts us and enables us to *release* emotionally. We also gain economic benefits, as we build relationships with clientele, coworkers, and customers, no matter how brief the meeting.

Young men are by far the greatest perpetrators of violent crime in our society. Their high levels of testosterone, coupled with inexperience and lack of wisdom, produce a powerful mixture of strength and naiveté that results in frequent violence. Interestingly, we see a dramatic decrease in violence in young men who have been raised in a home where physical touch was common. Young boys who are held, hugged, and given physical comfort and encouragement from their parents, are better off. They are psychologically stronger, wiser, and more secure than peers who did not receive this kind of upbringing.

All of the mass shootings we've had in our country over the past few years have been perpetrated by young men. I wonder what their upbringing was like, and whether or not they had loving homes? Almost every time I see violence in the news, it's a young man who committed the act. Over the last several decades, affection has become more accepted between fathers and their children, yet we still have homes where it isn't a part of daily life. We still see men who are uncomfortable telling their children that they love them. We must let our men know that expressing love demonstrates strength and honor. Their sons and daughters not only deserve this affection but also crave it and are better off with it.

Small touches do amazing things for relationships. They are a simple way to convey love and affection, without words or grand gestures. Touching your partner as you pass by them, conveys warmth, affection, and deeper messages of trust, connection, comfort, and attraction. A hand placed gently on a lover's shoulder can speak volumes, depending on the circumstance. It can mean support and unity as you deal with a struggling teenager. It might convey excitement and encouragement as your spouse is working on an important project. It could represent a secret reminder to talk about something important with friends or family during dinner, or comfort when a loved one has passed. You interpret these signals more specifically the longer you have been in a relationship. You also interpret them as you need to at the time.

Waitresses who gently touch customers on the shoulder when asking how their meal is, or if there is anything else they would like, typically get higher tips than non-touching wait staff. When shaking hands with clients, men who use two hands (one over, one under) convey warmth, trust, and honesty, and are more successful in business, than men who give unsupported, flippant, overly-aggressive, or casual handshakes. Physical contact and eye contact work hand-in-hand (pun intended) to convey positive messages when working with others.

Gentle, platonic touching, between teachers and students, improves not only the relationship between students and their instructors, but also student's learning ability, and interest in the subject. Students are more likely to raise their hand and ask a question, after having some small physical contact with the teacher. This may be because they have been "invested" in the teacher and a relationship with them, and they strive to please them by sharing an enthusiasm for the subject, and doing well.

Mindful human contact begins with consent and is always appropriate. Never force human contact, even with a child. Especially do not require a child to physically kiss, hug, or otherwise touch someone they do not want to (even grandma). It is important for them to know that their body belongs to them and that encroaching should not be tolerated.

Human touch is so powerful that it can heal our minds and bodies. Many hospitals are inviting massage therapists to give massages and mindful touch therapy to newborn babies, pregnant mothers suffering from particularly bad Braxton Hicks contractions, sick children, and adults in psychiatric wards. Hospice patients are utilizing massage therapy as well. Because human touch is so incredibly valuable, it is becoming another layer of treatment for the ill and is effective in easing the suffering of people who are terminally ill, even to the point of their passing. We all want someone there, holding our hand, in our final moments. Compassionate, mindful touch, can provide comfort and support, to anyone in need.

Physical contact with another person has also been shown to increase oxytocin levels. Known as the "love hormone," women who've recently delivered a child are brimming with it. More is released every time she nurses her baby, increasing the bond between them. Simply hugging another person increases this hormone in our bodies, leading to deeper relationships, and a desire to see the other person safe and well.

Post bath massage has a calming effect on nearly everyone. It's used to help babies and toddlers relax and sleep. Young children who suffer from hyperactivity or anxiety will benefit from massage, as will adults who are overwhelmed or stressed. Even a simple hug can be a tremendous help to a person who is struggling. Hugs relax muscles. They relieve tension, reduce headache pain, and alleviate both anxiety and stress symptoms. Heart hugs - full hugs where the hearts of two people seem to touch when held for an extended time, can raise serotonin levels and give us a happiness "boost." For children, heart hugs fill them with a sense of security and safety, while also giving them feelings of joy and happiness.

Danger knows when I'm stressed, and will rub my shoulders and offer extra hugs on those days. He's incredibly perceptive of my moods, and if they ever dip down, so I seem to be struggling, he's right there to offer his support, both physical and emotional. A quick back scratch, shoulder or neck rub, or just a hand on my back while I'm cooking, tells me that he's there for me. He sees that I may be struggling, and his touch shares his strength and support. I emulate his practice frequently because he's taught me so much about how to love someone through touch.

Your mindfulness practice

Used wisely and with care, touch can heal and benefit us in tremendous ways. We are blessed to have something so simple that can give us such great joy. A hug costs nothing, but is priceless!

Final Thoughts

You are enough, just as you are. You are right where you need to be right now. If you are on the cusp of change, I wish you strength and courage. If you are content where you are, I wish you more of what you have. If you struggle, my love and hope are with you, as are these chapters. Yes, this book is for you.

You are my neighbor, who suffered in the darkness of depression for months, without hope of light returning. You are my friend, who was overcome by grief when your husband died, yet found unknown strength for the sake of your children. You are the woman I saw in the store, quietly weeping and hoping no one saw her or overheard her painful phone call when she got the news. You are the mother, who struggles to get through the day when life seems overwhelming, or you are the older woman who is considering a change in faith or paradigm, and finally allowing herself to bloom.

You are me - a recovering anxious, sometimes overwhelmed

mom, just trying to present her family with more love, more patience, and more wisdom than the day before. Just a little better today than we were yesterday, that's us. We're the mountain climbers of humanity, taking one determined step after another, toward a goal of poise and grace, and yes...joy. It exists in this very moment. You've only to look to find it. You simply need to stop, look around, and notice the beauty and the joy that envelopes you every day. By acknowledging this joy, you also tell yourself that you are worthy of it.

You are worthy.

A Special Invitation

It started as a small group of close friends who wanted to keep up on my book writing progress. Then, a few encouraging acquaintances joined, and soon complete strangers. Every day, new people are joining the Unleash Joy community. They share personal stories, exciting news, uplifting messages. They encourage and uplift each other, all the while working through the 30 chapters of the book. Some having gone through it several times, and offering wisdom and guidance to those who are new.

I never expected the group to grow as fast as it has, nor for those who joined to be some of the most positive and uplifting people! It has become such a joy for me, as well as for the members, to see it grow and to experience the daily positivity and support. I am continually blown away by the heartfelt messages and loving acceptance that the group provides.

I warmly invite you to join the Unleash Joy community. Simply go to www.unleashjoy.com/community and request to join the

Unleash Joy Facebook Group. Here you'll be able to meet and connect with others who have read, or are reading the book, and working through each of the chapters. You'll find support, friendship and counsel from all over the world in this community! I personally moderate the group and will be checking in regularly, as well as posting uplifting messages of encouragement and support.

If you'd like to connect with me personally on social media, I invite you to follow me on Twitter @JaneenBrown, on Facebook https://www.facebook.com/janeenrbrown and on Instagram @unleash_joy.

Work with me! I offer one-on-one coaching services by phone or online via Zoom. To get on the waiting list for coaching, read my articles or view my courses, visit me at www.JaneenBrown.com. I look forward to connecting with you!

Before You Go

Before you go, I'd just like to say "Thank you." Of all the books on self-improvement you could have chosen, you downloaded or purchased this one. I'm honored and humbled that you read my work. Thank you so much for reading it all the way to the end.

I'd like to ask you, dear reader, for a tiny favor.

Could you please take a minute or two and write a review for this book on Amazon? Your feedback will help me to continue to write the kind of books that help to get the results you need. If you enjoyed the book, or if it helped or inspired you, please let me know!

Made in the USA
Middletown, DE
23 June 2017